MORE   PRAISE   FOR

My Joy, My Sorrow: Karen Ann's Mother Remembers

"The celebrated case of Karen Ann Quinlan is a landmark in American medical-legal jurisprudence. Indeed, the Quinlan case continues to inform and authenticate how we care for one another at the end of life and its prominent progeny includes: presidential and state bioethics commissions, the development of 'Living Will' Acts, the establishment of 'Ethics Committees' in our nation's health care institutions, Congress's Patient Self-Determination Act and the eventual federal funding of the National Hospice Movement.

"In *My Joy, My Sorrow*, Julia Duane Quinlan, Karen's mother, takes us behind the headlines and with unordinary grace, wisdom and humanity reveals an inspiring testament of faith and familial love. While Karen Ann innocently became the everywoman of the patient's rights movement, her family faced the tragedy of her illness and its consequent legal challenges with a heroic resolve found in the teachings and tenets of their shared Catholic beliefs.

"Julia Quinlan and her beloved and now departed husband, Joseph, used their accidental celebrity with noble and generous purpose. This book chronicles an American Catholic family's universal witness of the sacredness of human life and imparts a keener awareness of the inter-relationship between life and that death which awaits us all. This is the rich gift of *My Joy, My Sorrow* and its tender telling of the Quinlan saga."

—THE HONORABLE PAUL W. ARMSTRONG
Superior Court of New Jersey, and former legal counsel to the Quinlans during the landmark Quinlan decision

"...While partly the story of the first American icon of humanistic end-of-life care, it is also the story of a family that knew that open communication, faith, mutual respect and concern for one another would sustain them through this unprecedented experience....There is more authenticity in this book than in any I have read in years. Its debut at this controversial time makes it irreplaceable reading for anyone truly concerned about end-of-life care."

—DONALD L. PENDLEY, M.A., CAE, APR
President of the New Jersey Hospice and Palliative Care Organization

"In light of the polarization engendered by the [Terry] Schiavo case, this book of memories is more relevant than ever and also very helpful. American health care decision-making is becoming very technology dependent. 'If we can do it' the saying goes, 'we should.' Julia Quinlan's battles with the public and the courts give us hope that the Catholic tradition of 'allowing to die' is not forgotten in a fundamentalist world where 'life at all costs' is unfortunately seen as the heart of both religious and secular wisdom."

—MONSIGNOR JOSEPH W. DEVLIN
LaSalle University, Philadelphia

"…an amazing story of how a mother and a family coped with enormous challenges and heart-wrenching choices often in the face of public scrutiny and comment. No one who reads Julia Quinlan's account of her life could come away with anything but the deepest respect for a compassionate and often heroic woman. This book should be read by anyone who wants to better understand the impact of death and dying on families in America."

—ARTHUR CAPLAN

The Emanuel and Robert Hart Professor of Bioethics, Chair of the Department of Medical Ethics, and Director, Center for Bioethics, University of Pennsylvania, and author of several books on bioethics, including Moral Matters: Ethical Issues in Medicine and the Life Sciences *(John Wiley & Sons)*

MY JOY,
MY SORROW

KAREN ANN'S MOTHER REMEMBERS

• Julia Duane Quinlan •

ST. ANTHONY MESSENGER PRESS

Cincinnati, Ohio

Pulling the Plug...Is it murder or mercy? Ladies' Home Journal Poll. Copyright March 1976. Excerpted with the permission of LHJ, Meredith Corporation.

Excerpt from *Karen Ann: The Quinlans Tell Their Story* by Joseph and Julia Quinlan with Phyllis Battelle. Published by Doubleday. Used by permission of the publisher.

Photo insert of Julia and Joe Quinlan with letters taken by Steve Andrascik. Best attempts to contact photographer were made to receive permission to reprint.

Cover and book design by Mark Sullivan
Cover photo: AP/Wide World Photo

Library of Congress Cataloging-in-Publication Data

Quinlan, Julia Duane, 1927-
    My joy, my sorrow : Karen Ann's mother remembers / by Julia Duane Quinlan.
        p. cm.
    Includes index.
    ISBN 0-86716-663-0 (pbk. : alk. paper)
    1. Quinlan, Julia Duane, 1927- 2.   Quinlan, Karen Ann. 3.   Right to die. 4.   Terminal care—Moral and ethical aspects. 5.   Assisted suicide—Moral and ethical aspects. 6. Parents of terminally ill children—New Jersey—Biography. 7.   Coma—Patients—New Jersey—Biography.   I. Title.
    R726.Q563 2005
    179.7—dc22

                                                    2005007852

ISBN 0-86716-663-0

Published by St. Anthony Messenger Press
28 W. Liberty St.
Cincinnati, OH 45202
www.AmericanCatholic.org

Printed in the United States of America.

Printed on acid-free paper.

05 06 07 08 09 5 4 3 2 1

I dedicate this book to the memory of my beloved husband, Joseph, for fifty years of uncompromising love.

And to the memory of my beloved daughter, Karen Ann, my precious gift from God.

CONTENTS

ACKNOWLEDGMENTS

The idea for this book took root several years after the death of my husband. Being alone gave me time to think about my life and the life Joe and I shared.

It was several years later that I started to put my thoughts on paper. I had no organized thoughts; I jotted words down as they entered my mind. Frankly, my story changed direction several times.

As I began to put words and thoughts together, I realized that I had lived an incredible life and survived incredible experiences, both as a young woman and as an older adult.

Writing about issues that were deeply embedded in my mind and in my heart was an emotional experience. As I gathered words on paper, I knew this would be a difficult story to write. Many, many tears were shed. At times it was impossible to continue. However, I truly felt inspired to go on.

Many people helped to ease my journey, perhaps with a smile or a hug when I needed it most—maybe by redirecting my thoughts or giving me words of encouragement. But most of all they cared. All of these people hold a special place in my heart.

My heartfelt thanks to my daughter Mary Ellen for the many hours she spent reading chapter after chapter, making corrections and offering suggestions. She was my critic in a loving way.

Thanks to my son John for his endless encouragement. To both of my children for their patience in helping Mom achieve her goal. They are my source of strength.

I am fortunate to have the support and encouragement of the wonderful people at Karen Ann Quinlan Hospice—the staff, the board, professional team and volunteers. They were always there for me.

A special thanks to Tracy Sheptik, for sharing her thoughts on caring for Joe as a hospice patient. I'm sure it was difficult for her to put her thoughts on paper, but she did it with love and compassion.

Many thanks to Jane Brace, Bill Ehrhardt, Shelia Lacouture, Ray LaTour, Rich Pompelio, Jack Prather, Bob Romano, Colleen and Louis Ruggiero, Maureen and Marty Siebold. I am forever grateful for their continued encouragement. They each helped in their own unique way.

I am grateful to all the people who supported my family and me throughout our long ordeal. It was not just one person, but a community that extended beyond the boundaries of Landing, New Jersey. I heard their prayers. I read their letters and cherished them. The nation and the international community embraced the legal, ethical and medical decisions we made as a family. You were all very much in my thoughts as I relived my experiences.

I am deeply grateful to Lisa Biedenbach, Editorial Director of St. Anthony Messenger Press, for giving me the opportunity to write this book. I would also like to give special thanks to my editor, Mary Curran Hackett, for her guidance and encouragement. Lisa and Mary made themselves available to me, answering my many questions. They guided me every step of the way. I appreciate their recognizing that this is an important story. It has been a rewarding experience and a privilege to work with them and to be associated with St. Anthony Messenger Press.

FOREWORD

While some people liked to think of Karen Ann Quinlan as a "Sleeping Beauty," her mother Julia thought of her as "My Little Fighter." Karen Ann, who after a tragic accident survived the removal of a respirator but remained in a comatose state for ten years, was a fighter for all that time—she fought off the end of life in this world.

But Karen Ann's mother and father were fighters too, though in other and very different ways. They fought off many challenges to their own well-being. They went through the emotional stages that Doctor Elisabeth Kübler-Ross identified as normal experiences in facing the inevitability of death.

Joe and Julia Quinlan also fought off strong objections from many ethicists and theologians, jurists and medical experts when they followed through on what they and their other children, Mary Ellen and John, were sure was Karen Ann's desire that no extraordinary means be employed to keep her alive in a comatose state without any possibility of recovery.

Julia Quinlan's reflective account of her own life as she has lovingly lived it with her wonderful husband Joe, their adopted daughter Karen Ann and their two other children, as well as other family members and some very important people in her life, especially Father Tom (Monsignor Thomas Trapasso) and Attorney Paul W. Armstrong, is not a sequel to *Karen Ann* published in 1977 by Doubleday. *My Joy, My Sorrow: Karen Ann's Mother Remembers* is Julia's own story.

Julia's story resurrected in my mind a weekend in 1975 when Father, now Monsignor, Herbert Tillyer and I pored over media reports, opinions of legal and ethical experts and the teachings of the Catholic church, notably a statement of Pope Pius XII addressing an international Congress of Anesthesiologists in 1957, as they applied to Karen Ann and her parents' desire to do God's will in her regard. Bishop Lawrence B. Casey, bishop of Paterson, had assigned us to work on a pastoral statement regarding Julia and Joe's decision to request removal of the respirator that was considered necessary to keep Karen alive, a request that was denied by Supreme Court Judge Robert Muir, Jr., on November 10, 1975.

The church of Paterson was not silent on this matter. Following an unofficial but negative statement by someone in Rome, I was authorized to make it very clear that: "The Paterson Diocese supports the Quinlans' decision. Their action has the approval, sympathy and understanding of the diocese."

Bishop Casey's Pastoral Statement of November 1, 1975, was a teaching document and was very much his own, and he was rightfully proud of it, especially after Chief Justice Hughes quoted him at a great length in his decision of March 31, 1976, which reversed that of Judge Muir and held that "the life-support apparatus now being administered" to Karen Ann Quinlan could be withdrawn under three easily verifiable conditions.

The title of Julia Quinlan's beautiful story, *My Joy, My Sorrow*, brings to mind the opening words of Vatican II's *Constitution of the Church in the Modern World*: "The joys and hopes, the grief and anguish of the people of our time…are the joys and hopes, the grief and anguish of the followers of Christ."

We share in one another's joys and sorrows. We all experience them in our own lives. Our burdens are lightened when the Lord supports us, when we know that the Lord supports us and also when we read how the Lord has supported someone like Julia Quinlan who shares her story with us.

Life's joys are all the greater when we find the meaning of life's sorrow. The brook without its rocks would lose its song.

—*Most Rev. Frank J. Rodimer*
Bishop Emeritus of Paterson

INTRODUCTION

My Joy, My Sorrow tells a story that is very dear to my heart. It is a story of my family's love for our daughter and sister. It is as compelling today as it was in 1975. It is a story that needs to be told.

Thirty years ago my daughter Karen Ann was rushed to the hospital. She was not breathing. What happened that early morning of April 15, 1975, changed my life, my family's life and the lives of thousands of people.

Despite what many people say or believe, my beautiful, vivacious daughter died that night. Yet her withered body lived on for ten years. During that time we shared her life, as well as her dying, with thousands of people all over the world. She became special to many. She was the "Sleeping Beauty" they prayed for—the poster child for our dilemma with death. Her graduation picture was as recognizable in Japan, Mexico, England and most European countries as it was in this country.

Karen's short life was a gift to her family. For twenty-one years we shared her love, her disappointments, her heartaches and her contagious laugh. We would never give back a single moment.

With all my heart I wish Karen's tragedy had never happened. But it did. From that moment on I knew I had to move forward and fight for what I believed in.

I did not know at the time that we were entering uncharted waters. That the decisions we made as a family would affect the decisions you would make in the future concerning your own medical care. It would change the way we all look at death and dying. The New Jersey Supreme

Court Decision in the Quinlan case is now part of our country's history.

Many stories have been written about my daughter. Others can write about the accident, about her life and about her death. But no one else can write about the profound pain and anguish we shared as a family.

To this day it is impossible for me to imagine how difficult all this was for my other two children, Mary Ellen and John. They not only had to cope with the loss of their sister, but also with the loss of their privacy when just being teenagers in 1975 was difficult enough.

In order to write this story of love, I knew I would have to share my innermost feelings. I would have to give insight as to how my life experiences prepared this shy, quiet, young woman for those ten years and beyond.

My Joy, My Sorrow is not just a story of Karen's life or of her struggle; it is also a story of my life and my struggles. As I started to write, I had to ask myself, "Who am I?" I asked that question repeatedly. It was necessary for me to look deep into my childhood and my adult life and try to discover what made me the person I was in 1975. What gave me the strength and the courage to carry out my convictions? On the surface anyone who didn't know me or my past would say I lived an unremarkable life until that day in 1975. I came from an average family. I was neither the youngest nor the oldest. I was born at a time when jobs and money were not plentiful. I had an ordinary childhood, raised in an ordinary, small town. But there was so much more—so much that made me the person I was—the person I needed to be for Karen, Joe and my other two children.

There was no single instant that changed my life. Like

many, my innermost being was formed slowly over time and was fostered by the love of my parents and then of my husband. There was never a moment in my childhood or as an adult that I doubted my parent's love. I had this security to the end of their lives. I can only hope that they were as assured of my love in return. I also had an amazing life with my husband, Joseph. And our experiences together—as friends, lovers and then parents—shaped who I am as a person. I know I could not have written this story without the love of Joseph. His gentleness and love sustained not only me, but also our children throughout those difficult years and beyond. In addition, we sustained one another through love, patience, acceptance and understanding.

After Joe's death I had to search again; I had to ask that same question: "Who am I?" I don't ever want to stop searching or growing.

This will not be an easy story to read. It was not an easy story to write. Perhaps, you will shed tears, as I shed many tears in writing it. It is a beautiful story of a family's love. It is a story of deep love shared through happiness and adversity.

It is a story that I hold close to my heart. And I hope you will also.

PART ONE : OUR STORY

My Childhood

I was born and raised in a small town in New Jersey, called West New York. It sits across the river overlooking Manhattan, giving us a spectacular view of the New York skyline.

I attended St. Joseph's grammar and high school with my sister and two brothers. Although it was a time when jobs and money were scarce, we remained a close family. I had the advantage of growing up in the same town as my cousins. We played together, had fun on Saturday afternoons going to the movies or just hanging out. We remained close throughout our school years and into adulthood.

Many small events shaped me and readied me for my years in the public spectacle following Karen's accident. But nothing prepared me for my life under public scrutiny as much as walking with my mother when I was a young child. I used to love walking with her and holding her hand. Mama was tall, slender and beautiful, but as we walked, other children, as well as adults, would turn and stare at her. Mama had a very deep purple, black and red birthmark that covered the entire left side of her face. As a child these stares angered me. I wanted to shout, "Stop! Stop staring!" But I never did. All I could do was stare back. It had to be a very painful experience for Mama. I'm sure the stares hurt her deeply. But she never talked about it. She accepted it. She was the most caring and gentle woman I ever knew. As I matured, I learned to accept the stares. And I saw real beauty in my mother. With her acceptance she taught me an invaluable lesson. I tried to carry that throughout my childhood and into my adult life. Her quiet grace and dignity inspired me—and carried me through many ordeals.

When I was fourteen I met my future husband. He was tall, handsome and very shy. We lived in the same apartment building as his oldest sister and her family. Joe ("Buddy" was his nickname) would often babysit her two children on Saturday nights. That's how we met.

Joe was also born in West New York, although he grew up in a neighboring town. He was the youngest of six children. When Joe was twelve his father died, and that sad occurrence had an impact on him for the rest of his life. Joe often shared memories of his dad with me—how they would take long walks together holding hands. Joe loved watching games in the park or just talking to his dad. He cherished every moment. Later when we were married, Joe said he prayed every night that he would live to see his children grow up. He never wanted them to be without a father at a young age.

Joe had to leave school at the age of sixteen to help support his widowed mother. He went to work for Kaye Woody Pipe Factory in town. He worked on a machine and dreamed of the day when he could leave. At this time in his life, he had no choice.

It was very convenient for Joe and me to have his sister living upstairs. Suddenly, Joe was very anxious to babysit. He would leave the door to the apartment open, and we would sit on the stairs and talk. When I discovered he didn't know how to dance, I offered to teach him. He had good rhythm and was a fast learner. We'd play records and dance. It made the time pass quickly, sometimes too quickly. We both looked forward to those Saturday evenings.

Joe was very mature for his age. I was a teen enjoying my teen years. Joe had a special quality about him, a gentleness and thoughtfulness not usually found in the young. These qualities stayed with him all his life. Our friendship grew deeper as we shared our dreams and hopes for the future. I knew at that very young age that there would be no one else for me. Joe felt the same.

One thing led to another, and my parents finally allowed me to date Joe when I was fifteen. Often we'd ride the bus to Journal Square, Jersey City. There were two beautiful theaters, the Lowe's and the Stanley. They always had the latest movies. Other nights we'd go indoor rolling skating or just spend time strolling down Lover's Lane on Boulevard East. That was our favorite spot. For my sixteenth birthday Joe gave me a friendship ring. I still wear it every day, though the engraving has since worn away. It is my treasure.

World War II

As so many lives changed on December 7, 1941, ours did too. As usual I was listening to the radio. The music was suddenly interrupted. The announcer said, "President Roosevelt is going to address the nation." This was most unusual. My family and I gathered around the radio to listen. Then the president spoke, "My friends, this morning at 7:55 A.M. the Japanese bombed Pearl Harbor in a surprise attack and other military bases on Oahu. The attack lasted two hours." Then the stunning words, "We are at war." We listened to his words in silence.

I had no idea what war was really like. The horror and the loss of life were things I saw only in the movies. But this was real—it was not Hollywood. I had no idea how this infamous day would change my life. My thoughts turned to my brother Bill. He would have to register for the draft. As time passed, there were fewer and fewer young men in town. They all went willingly, eager to serve their country.

I continued going to school. Joe and I continued our romance, and we wanted to spend as much time together as possible. We both knew that eventually he would be drafted. Life went on as usual with minor inconveniences. No one complained—all anyone ever talked about was the boys in the service. When we read or heard about a young man missing or killed in action, it hit home. We were just a small town. The war continued, and more and more young men were drafted. As my classmates graduated, they either enlisted or were drafted. Patriotism was as high in our small town as it was all over the nation. But we were all united in the prayer that the war would end soon.

Joe wanted to enlist, but his mother would not sign the papers. In 1943, when he turned eighteen, he registered for the draft. Like the majority of young men, he was anxious to serve. On August 6, 1943, he was inducted into the army. When he left for boot camp, he promised to write. There were no commitments. Joe wanted me to enjoy my high school years and to date other men. I did, but Joe was always in the back of my mind.

When he finally came home on leave, I couldn't wait to see him in his uniform. I also had apprehensions. Had he changed? Would he still have the same feelings for me? When I saw him walk through the door, he looked ever so handsome. But he was my same shy Joe. As we embraced and kissed, we both knew our feelings for one another had not changed. They say absence makes the heart grow fonder. How true.

His leave was too short. I didn't want him to leave. He couldn't tell me when he would be home again. When he was scheduled to leave with his unit, he had a hernia attack. He was rushed to the hospital and operated on. When he recovered, he shipped out with the 335th Infantry.

We were fighting the war on two fronts, the Pacific and in Europe. Hitler and the Nazis were in the headlines every day. Still, the war seemed like a distant enemy.

As war continued, we found out that Joe was sent to battle areas in Germany and Belgium. I kept in touch with his family. One night Nana (Joe's mother) called. She sounded very depressed. This was out of character for her; she was an upbeat person, even-tempered and happy. "Julia," she said, "I have some terrible news for you." I know my heart stopped for a moment. I didn't know what she would say next. A horrible thought entered my mind: *Was Joe killed in action?* I was frightened to hear her next words.

She went on to say, "The small finger of his right hand was hit." Then a long pause. I could tell she was crying. When she spoke again, she said, "His left arm was blown off too." I don't remember if I answered Nana. I was in a state of shock.

Days later when we talked again, she was able to repeat to me her conversations with Joe. She had told him everything would be all right, and that she just wanted him to come home. "We all love you," she said. I know how I felt: hurt, angry, sad—all at the same time. I could not imagine how deeply Nana must have hurt.

Several days later when he called again, she told him that the Christmas tree was up and would remain up until he came home. The gifts would remain wrapped under the tree, waiting for him. It was a long wait. But that didn't matter. He was one of the lucky ones, and he was coming home.

After several days I was able to think clearly and many questions entered my mind. My first thought was gratitude that Joe was alive and would be coming home. I wondered if he would be able to accept the loss. What would the future hold for him and for us? I could not help but think our dreams were crushed that day.

Joe was sent to a hospital in Atlanta, Georgia, for rehabilitation. They fitted him with an artificial arm, with a hook to replace his hand. They taught him to drive a stick car (with no power steering, brakes or windows—everything was manual) on a steep hill, shifting gears with his right hand and holding the wheel with the hook. He learned to use the hook to pick up things and to dress himself. He learned to tie his shoelaces with only four fingers (try it sometime). They taught him well. He was discharged June 29, 1945. When he came home, he was totally independent.

Joe never complained. He was thankful to be alive.

When he was in the hospital, he saw men far worse off than he. Some without legs, some without both hands, some blind. Many emotionally damaged for life. They were young men, eighteen, nineteen, twenty years old, who had lost their youth on the battlefield. And many thousands of other young men did not come home.

Joe never wrote to me while he was in the hospital. I got my news from Nana and his sisters. I was anxious for him to come home and hoped that he would call me. How I longed to hear his voice. There was nothing but silence.

After many months he was released from the hospital. When he arrived home, he found the Christmas tree still standing and the gifts waiting for him. He also found Nana, his sisters and brothers-in-law waiting to shower him with their love.

I was not there. Joe was not ready to see me. He called many nights, but he couldn't gather the courage to visit me. He was afraid I would continue our relationship out of pity. There was no way I could convince him otherwise. The phone calls became more frequent. He would tell me how much he missed me, how much he still cared. However, he was not able to take the final step to come and see me in person.

I went on with my life. I graduated and was offered a job with a local bank. I worked a half-day on Saturdays, and often on my walk home I would visit St. Joseph's church and say a few prayers. One Saturday I was feeling deeply troubled by Joe's conversations, so I went inside the church and prayed for a very long time. I pondered many things. I knew Joe loved me. He told me often of his love from a distance. He had his fears. I could relate to that. I also had mine. I wasn't sure I could accept him as he was. How much had he changed? Could I truly love a man with an artificial arm and a hook for a hand? I was young and I needed my questions answered, too. I don't know how long I sat in that pew, praying for guidance—for Joe and for me. But somehow I knew God would answer my questions in his own time.

When I arrived home, I had a wonderful surprise awaiting me. Joe was there. He looked exactly as I remembered him, still handsome and still shy. He reached out to hold my hand and then held me in his arms. I looked at his arm, at the hook, but I knew I had to look deeper. We sat in the living room and talked. I knew I loved him, but I had to be sure my love wasn't laced with pity. I asked him to remove his artificial arm. I wanted to look at the stump, and I prayed that I would not find it distasteful. I looked at Joe; I looked at the stump and kissed it. We both knew that our love was deeper than any war injury. I grew up that afternoon and fell deeper in love with this wonderfully shy guy. We would face other obstacles together.

When Joe came home, he thought he would see other young men in town with war injuries, but he came across no one like him. He felt like he was a freak on display. One night we decided to go to New York City to have dinner and see a movie. We walked to Boulevard East and boarded the bus only to find it was crowded. There were no seats available. A nice man got up and said, "Here, soldier, take my seat. I can hold on." My heart ached for Joe. Instead of feeling honored, he felt shamed. The incident ruined a beautiful evening.

Other times we walked down the street and people would stare, turn around and stare some more. I know the stares hurt him deeply. But as I said earlier, Joe was a gentle man, and he never complained. One night when we were shopping for furniture, the salesman approached Joe, asked him what happened and then asked to see the hook. We couldn't get out of the store fast enough. Sometimes I felt anger and resentment. But once again someone I love taught me acceptance—an invaluable life lesson. Thankfully, Joe had an inner strength and confidence that gave him the courage to go on. Joe was not yet ready to talk to me about his war experiences. I never asked questions, because I knew someday in the future he would share the stories with me—when he was ready.

Joe's War Experiences

Joe didn't share these stories until many years later, but he believed these were the most crucial stories, in that they changed his life and his outlook forever. Like my mother's birthmark had prepared me for a life under public scrutiny, Joe's life—and his experiences with death during the war—prepared him for all of our own life-and-death battles.

During the war, he and his division had taken the little town named Sterling, Germany. When they pulled into town, their outfit was completely cut off from the other units by the German troops. The Germans had them surrounded. Every night these enemy soldiers would counterattack and try to infiltrate.

One night Joe was ordered to go on guard duty to watch approximately twenty enemy soldiers whom they had captured the night before. Joe was not alone in his duties. The other man assigned to the post was a Native American, and Joe was grateful he had him by his side. It was a difficult assignment and Joe didn't exactly feel at ease. He was only nineteen years old.

When they reached the site they were to guard, the prisoners were all sitting on the ground leaning against the wall of a stone building. He and the other guard didn't talk; they just concentrated on their duty.

Then a superior officer came out of the house that was being used as a temporary headquarters. The major called out to Joe and his partner, saying that he had just received word that the enemy was going to pull a counterattack that night.

"If that happens, soldier," he said to Joe, "I don't want any of these so-and-so's running around loose. I want you to kill every one of them, rather than letting them run around in the dark."

Joe couldn't believe what he was hearing. The major wanted him to be a firing squad. This was the first time he had faced this issue of morality. *Is it moral to kill unarmed prisoners?*

Many thoughts ran through his mind. He knew that in wartime to refuse an order meant facing a court-martial. Worse, to refuse an order meant jeopardizing the safety of not only one soldier, but also an entire infantry.

The other guard went over and sat down on a fence. But Joe had to walk. As he walked back and forth, he prayed so hard his lips were moving as fast as his feet. But he knew one thing right away: If the order came to kill all the men, he could not do it. He would die first.

Just before dawn two other young men came on guard duty to relieve Joe and his friend. Now he had to face another decision. Should he tell them what the major said and transfer his moral problem to them? No, he couldn't do that either.

He said, "The major says you may have a counterattack and if we do, don't let these prisoners run around loose. Those are the major's orders."

As it turned out a few minutes later, the Germans did counterattack and the replacements hustled every one of the prisoners down into the basement of a nearby building, where they spent the night. They were all safe. Joe couldn't help thinking that God's hand was in that, but certainly Joe's hand played a major role in it too—though he would never say as much.

Shortly after that experience, he was walking across an open trail with another young private. They were deeply engrossed in conversation, so close they almost touched each other. Suddenly, a sniper spotted the two easy targets and pulled the trigger. The sniper killed the fellow right beside Joe in mid-conversation. They fell to the ground together. The last sound the young private made was the last word he had said in his conversation to Joe, and as he died, the sound of the word got weaker and weaker, until it stopped altogether.

Joe was lying right alongside him and listening to him until the last breath was gone. All he could think of was, "God, why was I spared? Why is he dead, not me?"

Only a few days later, during the Battle of the Bulge, a third thing happened that affected him for the rest of his life and helped to seal his character.

During the battle there was a lot of noise and excitement, and Joe was scared and mad at the same time. The Germans began firing eighty-eight-millimeter artillery shells at them, and there was just no place to run and escape. Joe heard one coming and he headed for the ground. But the shell hit the ground in front of him and bounced up and caught him. He wasn't the only one. There were a lot of fellows around him screaming, and he started yelling and praying in the same breath.

That was when his arm was blown off and the small finger on his right hand was hit. He didn't feel any pain, but he was convinced he was going to die. He remembered his prayer was just, "No, Lord, not now, not here!" He kept screaming that over and over. He was scared and had a lot of life yet to live. He was only nineteen years old. A young officer came along and grabbed his arm and said, "Come on, let's get the hell out of here."

From that moment on Joe had a new appreciation for life, and the dignity and strength that it takes to live a life. He carried all these memories in his heart and did so bravely and honorably, just as he would handle all the crises in life that came his way. Joe felt that these experiences in the war, namely the ones in which God had spared him, had to be more than coincidences. Looking back, he felt that God was testing him and preparing him for a role in some larger plan.

Starting a New Life Together

With the war behind us, Joe and I were eager to begin our life together. We became engaged on my birthday and were married seven months later, September 22, 1946, in St. Joseph's Church, West New York, New Jersey. We traveled by train to Montreal, Canada, for our honeymoon. It was our first trip to that beautiful city. We wished it could have lasted longer, but we were also anxious to start our new life together in our newly furnished apartment back home in West New York.

After the war and despite his loss of a limb, Joe went back to work the machine at Kaye Woody. Resourceful as ever, Joe studied the machine, made some adjustments and had another machinist make some different parts so that he would be able to work as productively as before. He also took advantage of the G.I. Bill and enrolled in classes at City College in New York, studying business administration. He worked every day and attended school at night until he graduated.

I continued working at the bank. Like many young couples, we planned to have a family. I became pregnant, but at three months I had a miscarriage. The following year I had another miscarriage. Two years later I became pregnant yet again. After the third month I started to gain confidence. But at five months I lost that baby too.

To say it was a stressful time in our marriage would be an understatement. I became tense and fearful of trying again. This loss was devastating to me. Joe was very understanding and patient. We both wanted children but felt we would never be successful. We were happy, but that goal, that one missing ingredient we both wanted, seemed unreachable. We were not ready to talk about it.

A few years later we felt we had allowed enough time to pass in order to ease the hurt, and I became pregnant yet again. However, I still approached this pregnancy with apprehension. I searched out one of the best obstetricians in Margaret Hague Maternity Hospital in Jersey City. He gave me medication that he said would help me through the first few months until the fetus became larger. He was aware of my history and was being cautious. We both started to feel confident. I quit my job at the bank and rested as often as possible. Joe and I were living on cloud nine.

A Very Difficult Year
Several years prior to this pregnancy we had purchased a lot in Landing, Lake Hopatcong. We built a four-room bungalow that we planned to use as a summer hideaway.

When I became pregnant in 1953, we decided to leave West New York and make Lake Hopatcong our permanent home. Like most other families, we wanted our children to have many of the things growing up that we didn't have—like a backyard with swings and a sandbox.

Joe traveled every day to Kaye Woody. It was a long, tiring trip, and he had no desire to continue. He felt it was time to look for a position closer to home. The search turned out to be relatively short. He applied at Warner Lambert Pharmaceutical Company in Morris Plains, just thirty minutes from our home and was hired immediately. It was an exciting time for us.

We turned the spare room into a nursery. Not knowing the sex of the baby, we kept everything neutral. Decorating and planning for the future was exciting. We both were very sure that everything would be fine this time; after all I was in my ninth month. The doctor assured me the heart-beat was strong, and I knew the baby was very active.

A few weeks prior to my due date, my family gave me the long-awaited baby shower. It was thrilling to open all the gifts. I had enough diapers and nightgowns to last a long time. After the shower we drove to our new home with all the joy of parents-to-be. We put the gifts away, decorated the crib and dreamed of the big day.

The last week of my pregnancy, I stayed at my parents' home, so I would be close to the hospital. When contractions started the afternoon of July 28, 1953, we were very excited. Joe sped down Kennedy Boulevard breaking every traffic law. He wanted to be certain the baby would be born in the hospital—not in the car with him assisting.

When we arrived at the hospital, I was wheeled in, and Joe was left to fill out papers and answer questions. We kissed, and then I was taken upstairs to deliver our baby. I was young and didn't know what to expect. I found myself in a room with other mothers-to-be. They were all experiencing labor pains.

One woman had been there for many hours and was literally screaming. That didn't help to ease my concerns. I was in pain, too, but it was tolerable. A nurse came in to examine me. Then another nurse came in to listen to the heartbeat. Shortly after she left, another nurse came in, and she listened to the heartbeat. I asked if everything was all right. Their only answer was that the doctor would be in shortly. I began to get a sickish feeling in my stomach that everything was not all right.

When the doctor came in, he listened for a heartbeat. He listened again and again. I was terrified. He told me that I would have to do all the work and push with all my might. He told me that he feared the baby was dead.

"But the baby was alive and kicking when I arrived at the hospital. What could have happened in those few hours?" I pleaded with the doctor. I don't remember if he answered me. I don't even remember crying. I was in shock. I kept bearing down and pushing until our son was born. What should have been one of the most treasured events of our life turned out to be one of the saddest.

Then my thoughts turned to Joe. He was waiting these many hours for a nurse to tell him the good news. Waiting, I imagine, must have been difficult for him, for he had no idea what was happening. Finally, a nurse approached him. I could picture him standing there waiting for her to say, "You have a son," only to hear the most devastating words, "I'm sorry but your son was born dead. It was a stillbirth."

I never saw my baby. I never held Joseph Junior in my arms. When I awoke, I was in a room with a new mother who was nursing her baby. I was in a maternity hospital surrounded by happy mothers and happy babies. My roommate was very considerate of my feelings, however, and I was grateful that she never asked me to hold her baby.

When Joe was finally allowed to see me, he looked like he was still in shock. He tried to smile and comfort me, but neither of us felt like smiling. His main concern was for me. *Was I all right?* Yet I knew his heart was broken, too. Then he said, "I have a few details that I need to talk to you about. Since it was a full-term baby, we have to have him buried." A chill went down my spine. Then he went on to say that since the baby was not baptized he could not be buried in the Catholic cemetery next to my grandmother. Neither Joe nor I could understand why. But that was church law at the time. I cannot put into words the hurt that I felt. I looked at Joe—he was hurting as much as I was, but he was the one who had to make all the arrangements for our son Joseph. I could not help him.

He also had to break the news to my parents. When he arrived at their door my mother said, "When I saw Joe, I knew something terrible must have happened. He was shaking and was as white as a ghost."

I spent the next five days in the hospital. Each time that Joe visited he tried to make the conversation as light as possible by talking about everything except what was on both our minds—our dead baby. When we walked the halls, we made every effort to avoid the room where the newborns were. When Joe was not with me, I stayed in my room. There was no separate area for mothers who had lost their babies.

I left the hospital filled with sadness. The drive to my parents' home was difficult. I knew they were hurting for their daughter and for the loss of their first grandchild, and my sister was hurting for me and the loss of her nephew. But, they were so happy that I was okay. I stayed with them for some time. Mama cooked all my favorite dishes, while trying to cheer me up. I don't know what I would have done with out my parents' and sister's support.

We did not look forward to our follow-up visit with the doctor. What would his explanation be? The last time we drove down Kennedy Boulevard it was with excitement and anticipation, but on that particular evening it was different. Doctor Hall informed us that the baby died only hours before I delivered. He said that I was very small and

I would never deliver a live baby. I still did not understand what could have happened in those few hours. How could I have come into the hospital with a live baby and have him die in the delivery room? I asked myself the same question over and over. We were devastated to hear that the chance of having a baby was very slim.

I knew I had to share the news with my parents. Naturally, their concern was for me. They put up a brave front for my sake, and they did not ask many questions. No one ever mentioned "the next time."

Would there ever be a next time? Joe and I were not ready to make that decision. What hurt me more than anything was how deeply Joe was hurting. He didn't cry (like his wife did), he didn't curse, swear or scream. He kept it all in his heart. I could feel the pain every time I looked at him, every time he held me close. In 1953 men did not cry. Today, Joe would have cried.

Joe and I decided it was time for us to return to Lake Hopatcong. He had a new job, and his new employer had been very understanding. The drive back home was agonizing. We had looked forward to our first Christmas with our baby but had to face the emptiness. We also knew we would be burdened with the tasks of returning gifts, removing the crib and turning the nursery back to a guest room.

One gift was precious to me. My mother and father bought the baby a beautiful long white christening dress with matching booties and cap. I held onto it for a long time. One day I decided to gather up enough courage to return it. When I finally brought the dress up to the sales clerk, she told me she could not accept it as a return, because I had no sales slip and I had waited too long to bring it back. Then the saleslady asked me, "Why didn't you return it sooner?" I looked at her and said, "My baby died," then I cried uncontrollably. It was the first time that I admitted to myself or said aloud to anyone else that my baby was dead.

There were no grief recovery programs in 1953 (that I was aware of); there were no organized support systems for mothers like me. Nevertheless, there was Joe (the best support system I could ever have asked for), my wonderful family and my faith.

The holidays were approaching and we knew it would be a difficult time for us. Joe and I leaned on one another. He held me in his arms when I cried. I sat with him, as he grieved in silence. We did get through the holidays, and it strengthened our marriage and our commitment to have a family.

A Precious Gift

After the holidays we started talking about adopting a baby. I called Catholic Charities in Paterson, New Jersey, and they made an appointment for us to be interviewed. Our caseworker was to be Miss Helen Reed. The paperwork was started. What a wonderful way to start a new year! We told ourselves then that 1954 would be a memorable year.

About a week later Miss Reed phoned and requested we send a letter to Sister Naomi, administrator of St. Joseph's Children's Hospital and Maternity Hospital in Scranton, Pennsylvania. We did so immediately.

I checked the mailbox every day. *Would there be a letter from Sister Naomi? No, not today—hopefully tomorrow.* I was not discouraged. I knew she would respond to our request. But I wondered how long would we have to wait and what her answer would be. While we were waiting, we received a phone call from Miss Reed. She wanted to schedule a visit to our home for the following week. "Yes, that would be fine," I replied. When I got off the phone, so many questions went through my mind.

In 1954 Landing was not built-up. There were only a few homes on our street. I was concerned she might feel the area was too isolated for a child. Would she think we would make suitable parents? Was the house too small? Our future as a family rested on her all-important visit. I knew she would send a detailed report to Sister Naomi.

The visit was cordial and pleasant. She was pleased to find a separate room for the baby, a large front and backyard. It also pleased her that the Catholic school, Our Lady of the Lake, was only a few miles away. She did ask our reason for moving to Lake Hopatcong. I felt she was satisfied with our answer that we felt it was a suitable place to raise children. They would enjoy the amenities that the lake area offered both winter and summer.

Overall, it was a pleasant meeting. As she was leaving, she said she would arrange a meeting for us with Sister Naomi. We took that as a positive sign. Despite all the telltale signs that we had reasons to hope, we tried hard to curb our enthusiasm, lest we be disappointed yet again. We knew the meeting with Sister would be the determining factor.

Miss Reed scheduled a meeting for early February. We anxiously waited for that day. When it arrived, it was filled with apprehension. The ride to Scranton was tense. We had no idea what questions Sister would ask.

When we arrived, Sister Naomi greeted us at the door.

She seemed very pleasant. After some light conversation, she started the interview. She asked questions about our childhood, our marriage and our faith. She mentioned that she received a beautiful letter from Father Duffy, pastor of Our Lady of the Lake Church, telling her that we were a couple with deep religious faith. "That means a great deal to us," she said. The interview lasted several hours. When it was over, she thanked us for coming and we thanked her for the interview and said that we looked forward to hearing from her.

The drive home was tense. "How do you think we did?" I asked Joe.

"I don't know," he replied. "It was difficult to judge; she asked so many questions."

Neither of us felt like we knew what the result would be. All we knew was that we were honest and forthright with our answers. The next few weeks would be a time for waiting and praying.

Time passed slowly. I had heard of couples waiting months, sometimes a year, before they received any encouraging news. So I was surprised and overjoyed when Sister Naomi called just six weeks later.

"I have a child ready for you. Could you come tomorrow to pick up your baby?" she asked.

Without hesitation and without speaking to Joe, I said an emphatic, "Yes, Sister, we will be there!" Then I called Joe at work to tell him the good news.

"Is it a boy or a girl?" he asked.

"I don't know. When Sister said, 'pick up your baby' I was so excited that I neglected to ask!" We both started to laugh.

It was a very happy moment for the both of us. We attended Mass in our parish church in the morning, and then stopped at a store on the way to Pennsylvania to buy something to bring our baby home in.

When we arrived, Sister Naomi met us at the door.

"Good morning, Sister."

"Good morning, Mr. and Mrs. Quinlan. Thank you for coming so soon."

Then she took us to a small chapel in the hospital. We knelt at the altar in front of the statue of our Blessed Mother. It was here in the chapel that Sister placed a baby wrapped in a blanket in my arms. She then said "although this baby comes to you through us, she is a gift from God."

Little did I know back then, truly, what a gift from God her life would be to the entire world.

She was the most beautiful baby, with a little tiny nose and ears and big blue eyes. I could not believe that I was holding our baby. Joe and I prayed together at the altar and gave thanks to God for blessing us with this precious gift.

I also gave thanks for her birth mother. It had to be very painful for her to give up her child. From what we were told by the sisters, she was a young woman of Irish descent. She was a parish secretary and a devoted Catholic. The young man that fathered our baby was of German heritage. That was all that the sisters shared with us about our child's birth parents. I prayed that somehow in the birth mother's heart she would know that she made a young couple so very happy.

We were now a family.

Our little girl was born March 29, 1954. We received her April 28, 1954. We named her Karen Ann. Joe and I were both overwhelmed with joy.

Joe drove very slowly going home. He kept turning and asking, "Is Karen all right? Should I slow down?" He was now the worried father.

When we arrived home, my mother and sister greeted us at the door. Mama was anxious to hold her first grandchild. My sister Alberta was anxious to hold her godchild.

The next morning I noticed Karen's eyes were not as bright as they were the day before. She looked like she might have been experiencing pain. Then she developed diarrhea and a high fever. I sat with her through the night. The following morning she was no better and was dehydrated. I called Joe and asked him to come right home. I called Doctor Morley Wells, a pediatrician in Dover that was recommended to me. I bundled her up, and as soon as Joe arrived, we rushed her to the doctor's office.

When he weighed her, he became alarmed. She had lost almost a pound from her birth weight. He immediately telephoned St. Joseph's Hospital. They told Doctor Wells that there had been an epidemic of dysentery among their babies and one of them had even died. But they were sure, however, that our baby got out in time. Well, our little Karen did not get out in time.

Doctor Wells rushed Karen to St. Clare's Hospital in Denville and placed her in isolation. She was given water and food intravenously through the veins in her forehead. We spent three days and nights at the hospital. My baby looked so tiny and helpless. And we felt helpless.

"I can't give you any hope," Doctor Wells said. We had expected the worse, but we still hung on to some hope. We had to. It was one of the darkest days of my life.

During this time Joe was in the process of becoming a confirmed Catholic and was attending confirmation classes at our parish (for reasons Joe never explained to me, he did not receive this sacrament in his youth). Nevertheless, on this particular evening and with Karen so sick, Joe was scheduled to receive his confirmation.

Joe didn't want to leave Karen's side. But I also knew how much being a confirmed Catholic meant to him. Doctor Wells assured us there was nothing either of us could do for our baby now. "Just pray," he said. So we did. We finally left the hospital—and we prayed—we prayed for our dying baby while attending Joe's confirmation Mass.

But before we left for church, I said good-bye to my new baby, whom I had loved from the first time I held her in my arms. I had Karen for only a short time but my love grew deeper as I walked the floor with her during the night, as I changed her diapers, bathed her, fed her, cared for her—as I learned to be her *mother.*

I don't believe I ever prayed as hard as I did that day in church. After Joe's confirmation ceremony we rushed back to the hospital. As Joe drove, I wondered how either of us could accept another loss.

When we arrived at Karen's room, Doctor Wells was standing at her door. He was a big man—over six feet, five inches tall—but kind and gentle. As he approached us, I felt weak and held on to Joe.

He said, "I don't understand it, but Karen has passed the crisis. She seems to be perking up."

I don't remember if I laughed or cried from joy. We had placed our baby in God's hands, and he truly blessed us.

As I stood by her bed, I said, "God has given you a second chance in life, Karen. He has also given me a second chance." My baby became more precious to me that evening than life itself. I looked at my baby and just thanked God for this miracle. Three days later we brought our baby home. Her eyes were bright again. She was able to keep food down. She was now the happy, lively baby we had brought home just a week before.

Miss Reed, our caseworker, visited us six months later. She was amazed to see how Karen had grown and that she could even stand while holding onto a table. Karen was a very active child. She didn't bother to crawl; she just got up and walked. And she loved to climb. In the evenings she looked forward to our quiet time together. I would sit her on my lap and read to her. Often she would pick up a book and pretend she was reading to me. Then came the hugs and goodnight kisses.

Suddenly, the void Joe and I had felt for so long was now filled with love and laughter. We were truly blessed.

(TOP) Joe and I on our wedding day.
(MIDDLE LEFT) Karen Ann's bright eyes and beautiful smile clearly project her happiness.
(MIDDLE RIGHT) Karen Ann loved to play with Mamie, the family's favorite cat.
(BOTTOM) On April 28, 1954, our marriage was blessed with a special gift. Karen was first placed in my arms at the altar in the chapel of St. Joseph's Church, Scranton, Pennsylvania.

(ABOVE) Karen was happiest when she was active. She was a born athlete. Here she is practicing her racquetball swing at Morris Catholic.

(TOP RIGHT) Karen and I on the day she received her First Holy Communion.

(BOTTOM RIGHT) Mary Ellen and John with their big sister (age nine) enjoying one of many family trips. This one was to Williamsburg, Virginia.

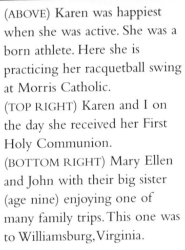

(TOP) Karen Ann Quinlan Center of Hope
Hospice—a dream fulfilled. It is my life's
dedication and a legacy of Karen.

(BOTTOM) John and Mary Ellen with me when I
was presented the 1999 Spirit of Hospice Award
by New Jersey Hospice and Palliative Care
Organization. It was a proud night for hospice
and for me.

(TOP) This beautiful photo of Karen was not only my treasure, but it became the world's as well. Today it is still internationally recognizable. (BOTTOM) Joe and I reading some of the thousands of letters we received from people all over the world. We read every one. They were all letters of support and prayers for Karen and our family.

PART TWO : THE FAMILY

The Formative Years

A FEW MONTHS AFTER KAREN CELEBRATED her first birthday, we decided to apply for a second child from Catholic Charities. Soon after, I discovered I was pregnant. I was torn between feeling happy and fearful. Was I strong enough physically and emotionally to go through that experience again?

I approached the pregnancy with great apprehension. I remembered the words of Doctor Hall, "You are too small. You will never have a successful pregnancy." I was fortunate to find a wonderful gynecologist, Doctor Emile Hornick. I called and made an appointment. In the meantime, he sent for my medical records. He examined me and then sat and talked to Joe and me.

"Do you realize that you have a negative RH factor, Mrs. Quinlan?"

"No, I was never told that," I replied.

Obviously, this was the real reason for my baby's still-birth and my miscarriages. I was shaken, realizing that this could happen again.

He patiently explained to us that new hormonal drugs should enable me to carry the fetus and deliver naturally. However, he said it is quite possible that I would have a "blue baby." He then assured us that even that shouldn't be a critical problem. He said he would prepare the hospital for an emergency blood transfusion for the baby as I neared full term. This was the first time I had ever had a doctor explain to me in detail what happened and what could happen. I felt very fortunate to have found him.

As May approached, the doctor felt I was ready and said he wanted to induce labor. We both agreed. When I arrived at the hospital, I was wheeled to a private room. This time Joe was not asked to leave. He stayed with me until they brought me into the labor room. How different from my last experience!

I was not in labor long. I was still hazy when Doctor Hornick said, "You have given birth to a beautiful baby girl. She weighs eight pounds, four ounces." I didn't believe him. I said, "Please don't lie to me. I know the baby is dead." I was reliving my last experience. I had convinced myself that the baby would be stillborn.

It was not until they brought the baby to me and placed her in my arms that I was convinced. She had this big clump of black hair and chubby cheeks. It was still hard to believe I was holding our beautiful daughter. She was born May 3, 1956, fine and healthy. We named her Mary Ellen.

What a joy it was to hold this precious gift in my arms! Her father stood there in disbelief, overwhelmed with joy.

The reality of having two daughters was just starting to set in. Now I was getting anxious to go home, to hold Karen again and again, to tell her how much I missed her and loved her.

When I came home and introduced Karen to her sister, she was not very impressed—she had wished for a brother. Just sixteen months later, her wish was granted. On September 28, 1957, I gave birth to our son, John, nine pounds, ten ounces. I truly couldn't believe it. John was such a big baby that he looked like he was three months old.

I will always be grateful to Doctor Hornick for his care, sensitivity and compassion. He assured me that he would be there for me and he was.

My two girls were different in many ways. Mary Ellen was quiet; she loved to play with her dolls, make tea and do all the things you expect little girls to do. Karen, on the other hand, loved to climb, run, play ball and participate in all sports. Consequently, there was little competition between them.

When a couple becomes parents, their perspective on life changes. Their love for one another is expressed in different ways, sometimes deeper, more meaningful ways. Their children become the bond that brings them closer together. Their life is centered on family. They become like a circle; there are no sharp edges. I was now able to relate to many of the concerns my mother had raising the four of us. It made me have a deeper appreciation for my parents.

My parents loved to spend time with their grandchildren. Almost every weekend they would take the bus from West New York to Hoboken, then board a train to

Landing. Joe would pick them up on a Friday evening after work. The children looked forward to the fun time with Grandma and Grandpa. When they were growing up, we had plenty of snow. My father would sleigh ride down Ryerson Road with them. He enjoyed it as much as the kids. My mother would play the piano and sing. She loved to play card games with them and taught them to play checkers. Mama was the indoor type. Papa was generally outdoors, taking long walks and getting to know the neighbors. Like most grandparents, they loved to spoil their grandchildren. But it was a joy to watch them.

I was what they now call a stay-at-home mom, and I loved it. Having three babies to care for was a full-time job. When Joe came home, he would pitch right in. He'd play with his daughters, bathe them and get them ready for bed while I fed John and prepared dinner. Sometimes the roles were reversed. He would hold his son and give him the bottle, while I bathed the girls. Joe was also very good at changing diapers, too. It was a very busy, happy time for us. After the children were tucked in for the night, it was quiet time for Joe and me. There were many evenings when we could not believe how our lives changed in three and a half short years.

Before we knew it, Karen entered first grade at Our Lady of the Lake School. Two years later, Mary Ellen followed, then John the next year. They walked to the bus stop together and back home together. As they neared the house, Karen would run ahead of her brother and sister, each wanting to be the first in the house to tell me what happened in school or on the bus. After a snack and change of clothes, they were outdoors until dinnertime, followed by homework.

We had a large backyard with swings and slides—all the necessities of a child's world. When they weren't in the backyard, they would ride their bikes in the driveway. As they grew older they were permitted, one by one, to walk to the ballpark, which was only a block away. Karen and her brother spent many hours playing on the field. In the summer we spent our afternoons on the beach.

It was a wonderful place for the children to grow up. Our children truly had the best of both worlds—a home to live in and a vacation-like location.

As the children grew, our home grew with it. We had the roof raised and added four rooms and a bath. Joe and his three helpers—Karen, Mary Ellen and John—completed the interior. I was the "gofer." It was a great family project. A few years later we added a large family room and a fireplace.

I became very much involved in the children's school—volunteering as class mother and as a chaperone during playground duty and class trips. It gave me the opportunity to meet their friends and other parents. I also became involved with the Brownie troop that Karen and Mary Ellen belonged to.

Joe became involved with Boy Scouts. He would go on camping trips to Allumuchy with John, winter and summer. It was a wonderful way for father and son to bond. Often the girls had sleepovers at friends' homes or at our home. John and his friends usually played ball. They were average children, busy with school activities and studying piano. Later John became interested in the drums. The house was filled with music.

Karen was in the first graduating class at Our Lady of the Lake School. Then she went on to Morris Catholic High in Denville, followed eventually by her sister and brother.

Three Teens
Karen joined the ski club, tried out for cheerleading and played racquetball. At sixteen she had her first date. She and a boy from school dated exclusively for several years. Mary Ellen dated a wrestler, and John joined the wrestling team (he was still too young to date). We were a busy family. There was an in-house joke that whenever I turned the ignition key the car would automatically go to Morris Catholic. It was a happy time in my life watching them mature and enjoying their teen years.

When Karen was old enough to drive, she bought a used Volkswagen Beetle. She loved driving around town in her very own Bug. Often she drove her sister to her after-school job at Buxton's (a local ice cream parlor) and drove her home. As they both matured, the two-year age difference was no longer important. They were able to relate to one another's feelings and to share stories about school and boys.

On September 22, 1971, Joe and I celebrated our silver wedding anniversary. We had a few friends and family over for dinner. The highlight of the evening for me was when Karen sang "Bridge Over Troubled Water," accompanied by her sister. Karen had a beautiful voice. It brought back memories of her singing at the Midnight Mass for Christmas as a child.

After Karen graduated high school, she chose not to go to college. It was a disappointment to her father and me. Like most parents, we just wanted more for our children than we had, and at the time college seemed like something we wanted more than she did. We could not change her mind. The summer after high school Karen took a job as a counselor at St. Regis Camp on Long Island.

When the camp closed, she came home and searched for a job. A family friend owned a service station in town and happened to mention to Karen that he was looking for full-time help. This excited her. She loved to putter around cars and that job would give her the opportunity to work with the mechanic. Her father and I were not enthusiastic about the idea; however, she needed the work. It was close to home, and we knew the owner. Karen was a quick learner and enjoyed every aspect of her job.

While she was working there, she learned of a family that lost their home and everything they owned in a house fire. A few people in town formed a committee to ask for donations. When Karen heard about it, she donated her entire week's paycheck. She said she could cut back on her own expenses. She never knew the family, but this action was typical of my daughter's generosity.

After a year or so at the service station, she wanted to move on and do something different. She got a job at a plastics company performing experiments. It was another challenge for her. She found the work to be interesting and rewarding.

Karen kept in touch with her close friends from high school. Often they would go to the city to see plays. She loved the theater. Always after seeing a play, I would hear her singing the following day. I remember so well her singing the songs from *Pippin* or *Jesus Christ Superstar,* or whatever plays she had seen.

Karen worked at the plastic company until it started to downsize. She was one of the last to be hired, so she was one of the first to be laid off. This did not get her down, however. She always had a positive outlook on life. If things did not go as planned, she would pick up the pieces and start over again.

About this time a friend of Karen's, Robin, needed a place to stay until she found an apartment. She asked Karen if she could stay at our house. We knew her and had no objections. Karen was willing to share her bedroom with her friend. And the arrangement worked out well.

Around this time a friend introduced Karen to a young man. He was a freelance photographer. They dated and the relationship appeared to be becoming serious. He was a nice, young man. We enjoyed his company and he enjoyed ours. Everything was going smoothly until he asked Karen to marry him. She was not ready to settle down, and they went their separate ways, though they remained friends.

Robin stayed with us until the end of 1974. She found a small house for rent on the lake and asked Karen to move in with her, so they could share all the expenses. Karen was not working but was collecting unemployment while she looked for a job. The house needed of a lot work. They painted, decorated and even repaired fixtures. When it was completed, it was lovely. They did a great job.

At the time John was still in high school and Mary Ellen was attending Centenary College. She often went over to Karen's after classes. They both loved to read and would discuss the books they read as well as the poetry they wrote. Karen shared her thoughts and her dreams with her sister. They were growing closer and realized how much they had in common. Their friendship and love for one another grew deeper as the months passed.

Gradually, Joe and I noticed a change in Karen. She seemed more mature and talked more about her future and wanted to join her sister at Centenary College to study voice and music. We both felt that Karen's move out of our house as well as her friendship with her sister had had a positive effect on her. Unfortunately, the owner of the house she and Robin were living in sold the property, and they were forced to move out. Robin went to live with her mother and Karen moved into a large house in Sussex with some other friends. She rented a room from them and lived there for what would turn out to be less than two weeks.

Karen Turns Twenty-One
On March 29, 1975, we celebrated Karen's twenty-first birthday. It was a nice evening shared with a few of Karen's friends and her grandparents. We all ate Karen's favorite dish—baked ziti and mozzarella.

Several days later I talked to Karen for a long time over the phone. Little did I know it would be our last conversation and the last time I would ever hear her voice and infectious laughter.

PART THREE : LIFE CHANGES

The Accident

OUR BUSY LIVES CONTINUED. WE WERE just an average suburban family enjoying our home and our children. We were unobtrusive people known only in our parish and small lake community. Our lives centered around home, family and church.

That is until the early morning of April 15, 1975, when we received a phone call in the middle of the night. The call that every parent dreads.

"Mrs. Quinlan, this is the nurse from Newton Memorial Hospital. Your daughter was admitted to the intensive care unit. She is unconscious."

Our only thought was that she had been in a car accident. Why else would she be in the ICU? Although Joe drove as quickly as possible, the drive seemed to last an eternity.

When we arrived, the doctor was waiting for us. He had questions to ask me, I had questions, too. But they could wait. At that moment I just wanted to see my daughter. As I entered the unit and looked at her, I noticed that there was a nasal gastric feeding tube in place and a tracheotomy. Both would remain in place until her death. It was unsettling to watch her struggle to breathe while I stood by helplessly.

Mary Ellen and John rushed to be at their sister's side. It was devastating for them to see her in that terrible condition. "She is in a coma," the nurse told us. "Talk to her. It may help."

We talked. But there was no response.

There was a moment when I felt that she knew I was there. I'm sure she felt my presence. The doctor asked many questions: "Was she on drugs?"

"No, she was not!" I responded.

I felt anger, but I knew it was important for them to know as much as possible about the chain of events that left Karen in a coma and unable to breathe on her own.

According to her friends, Karen was dieting to fit into a smaller size bathing suit. She had had nothing to eat all day. That evening they went to a local hangout for a few drinks to celebrate a friend's birthday. Karen had a few gin and tonics and then started to nod off. They drove her home and she went upstairs to lie down. Much later someone checked on her, and she was not breathing. This person tried CPR while waiting for the ambulance to arrive, but the CPR was not successful. A medic was able to resuscitate Karen and rushed her to the hospital.

When she arrived at the hospital, every means was used to save her life. Extraordinary means must always be used, for life is a precious gift. Early urine and blood samples taken on the day she entered the hospital, revealed only a "normal and therapeutic" level of aspirin and the tranquilizer Valium in her system. On the same day tests were taken for harder drugs (cocaine, barbiturates, inhalants, etc.). All the tests came back negative—which meant Karen had no drugs in her system. The doctors were flustered. They could take no remedial steps to arouse Karen from the coma if it wasn't drug-induced. All they could do was stabilize her breathing and place her on the respirator. The only thing we knew was that she was without oxygen for five, possibly ten, minutes. I sat at her bedside helplessly watching my beautiful child struggling to release herself from the machine that was breathing for her. Each time air was pumped into her lungs she grimaced.

"How much pain are you feeling, Karen?" I asked. She could not answer. I stood helplessly by and prayed for some answers. But there were none.

Many years later Mary Ellen shared her experiences, thoughts and feelings with me.

> The first time I went to see Karen in Newton Memorial Hospital, the intensive care unit nurse questioned me intensely.
>
> "Only close relatives are permitted in. How do I know you're related?" Finally, unsatisfied but realizing I wasn't going to leave, she said, "Go ahead. If you like to see people like that."
>
> Not especially liking to see people like that, particularly the person I most relied on to live forever, I went in anyway.
>
> Much later thinking about my first look at Karen in the hospital bed, her blood from the emergency trachea

just done splattered on the white sheets and pillow, I understood the attitude of the ICU nurse. Karen was one of their failures, in a world where technology replaces comfort and caring, where organs are transplanted from the dead so the living can cling to life and the business of medicine is managed by strangers. Karen was beyond help. Somebody no one wanted to look at.

Four months after my first look the world looked. A long, terrifying look at the value of life and its qualities. The void between caring and curing. The extraordinary distance medical technology will go before admitting failure. As the lines were drawn between machines and medicine, law and justice, life and death, the world couldn't look away. For the next ten years, we couldn't either. (Mary Ellen Quinlan-Forzano, 2004).

John was very close to his sister as well. Karen Ann was very athletic and loved to play sports with him. In his eyes she was strong, and he felt adamant that she would come out of the coma. After John first visited Karen, the color drained away from his face as though someone had slapped him with whitewash. He could not believe this was the sister who he played baseball and football and wrestled with. It was a terrible shock for him. Something he said he would never forget.

Nine days later the neurologist suggested that Karen be transferred to St. Clare's Hospital in Denville. Every available test was done. But all the results came back inconclusive or negative.

I sat at Karen's bedside day and night and watched her grimace as though she was in pain. The doctor assured me she was not. But I was not convinced. To stand by and watch a child suffer is difficult for any parent. I just wanted to take her pain away. By this time Karen's hands and feet were flexing, and her knees and elbows were bending inward. Each day it seemed her hands were clutched more tightly together. I watched as she returned to an almost fetal position. The prognosis was discouraging. Her coma was irreversible, and she was in a persistent vegetative state. There was no reasonable possibility of her returning to a cognitive, sapient state.

She was then moved from the center bed of the ICU to the end of the unit, apart from the activity. The therapist no longer came in. It was as though the medical community had given up. But I had not. The sight of my daughter suddenly shoved aside was disheartening.

Joe and I continued our daily visits. Our dear friends brought dinner to us nearly every night. Sometimes we were invited to their homes for dinner, and then we would go back to the hospital to say goodnight to Karen. Perhaps, I thought, one night she would feel my kiss. My intellect told me she couldn't, but my heart still had hope. Every day was filled with stress, but we were too numbed by what was happening to realize we were exhausted.

Coming to Terms

By late May, 1975, I faced the reality that there was no medical help for Karen. The time that the respirator could help her had passed. I began to question myself as to why she was still on the machines. I felt that now the emphasis should be on caring for Karen in a more compassionate way. In a way that would be good for Karen, not just those who did not want to let her go. Loving support was more important and humane than life-preserving, death-defying procedures. I could not share my feelings with my family; they were not prepared to listen to any hints that she might not recover. I tried to approach the subject with Joe. But each time he became very tense. His faith was very strong, and he truly believed God would perform a miracle.

I wish I could say my faith was as strong as Joe's, but it wasn't. I questioned God. I asked repeatedly, "Why? Why?" As my anger grew louder and stronger, I could not stop the tears. I felt terribly alone. I vowed I would never pray again. I was losing my faith and trust in God. I shared my feelings with my spiritual adviser and dear friend, Father Tom. He assured me that I *was* praying and that my anger and my questions were prayers. I was turning to God for help, and God was listening. This wonderful priest sat with me often as I cried openly and shared my innermost thoughts. I don't know what I would have done without him.

It was a confusing time for all of us, not just for Joe and me. John and Mary Ellen had thoughts of their own. Mary Ellen told me some time later, "I didn't really understand at first why we were going to turn off the machine. It was kind of a shock when you first suggested it. I couldn't think about what Karen would want the way you did." She had her own memories of Karen and her own experiences with Karen in the coma. She once shared her thoughts:

> One morning when I went down to Newton Memorial Hospital, something unusual happened. They [the nurses] always said to talk to her. I had called her name before and nothing had happened. She had these dead eyes. But I called "Karen," and she looked at me. It just happened once. I will always think she recognized me.

I skipped my classes and stayed around the hospital until ten o'clock that night waiting for her to look like that again. But Karen just returned right away to that blank stare. She never did look like she recognized me again.

I kept thinking about the time when I had pneumonia, and my mother put me in Karen's bedroom because the heat came up faster in there. Her room was always warmer than mine. Karen wasn't supposed to come in because she might catch my germs. But every night she'd sneak in anyway and sit on the side of my bed and tell me stories and rub my head until I went to sleep.

That night I think I realized she might die. And I remembered a nightmare I had so very long ago. In my dream I was getting married. I was standing in the back of the church; I kept looking around for Karen, but she wasn't there. Everybody else was—Mom and Dad, John, Grandma and Grandpa—but Karen wasn't in the church, and I ran down the aisle desperately looking and crying. "Where's Karen? I can't get married without Karen." But I couldn't find her anywhere.

When I woke up, I was scared. I sneaked into her room, and there she was in bed, sleeping, and I was so relieved.

Gradually, Mary Ellen recognized the futility of the machines. Then John accepted the fact that his sister was not going to make it. My husband Joe was the last holdout. But it was important that I allow him to reach this horrendous decision in his own time and in his own way. After months of prayer, discussion and spiritual direction with

Father Tom, Joe realized the truth and accepted the fact that there was no medical help for Karen. He recognized the futility of modern-day technology in our situation.

A Family's Decision

After many family discussions we asked to have Karen removed from the respirator and the cessation of all extraordinary means to preserve her life. It was the most difficult and heart-wrenching decision that we, as a family, ever had to make. Yet in our hearts we knew it was the right decision. We knew it was what Karen would want, had she been able to express her feelings. When I looked back on that day, I truly don't know how we got through it. I guess we just leaned on one another for strength.

My husband signed the authorization papers at the hospital, granting them permission to discontinue all extraordinary means, including the respirator. When I left the hospital that day, all I could think was that Karen's ordeal was over.

How wrong I was.

Two days later the hospital pulled out of the agreement, stating that Karen was twenty-one years old, therefore of legal age. Her father would have to go to court to become her guardian. What followed is history.

PART FOUR : THE LEGAL BATTLE BEGINS

BECAUSE KAREN WAS UNEMPLOYED at the time of the accident and not living at home, she was eligible for legal aid.

I clearly remember the day my husband visited Paul Armstrong in his Morristown legal aid office.

Joe was there to ask Paul to represent us in an unusual case. He was requesting legal permission to allow his daughter Karen Ann to die in peace, free of modern-day technology. We had no idea that we were about to enter uncharted waters.

On September 12, 1975, our attorney filed papers at the courthouse in Morristown. Judge Robert Muir was to hear the case. The trial was set for October 20, 1975.

We were advised to have our phone number unlisted. I couldn't understand why. We were only trying to do what was best for our daughter. How could anyone have a problem with that?

The following morning when I picked up the newspaper the headlines read, "Father Asks the Court to Allow

Him to Kill His Daughter." When John came downstairs, I was crying.

John asked, "What is the matter, Mom?" Then he, too, read the paper in disbelief. He sat next to me on the stairs and tried to comfort me. Neither of us could understand why anyone would print such a headline without knowing the circumstances.

From that moment on our lives would never be the same. We were literally thrust into the public eye. The privacy that we cherished was totally lost. Soon Karen's graduation picture was on the front page of every newspaper and magazine. Soon her picture was as recognizable in foreign countries as it was here in the United States. Reporters filled our home. They camped on the lawn, hid behind bushes and were always ready to snap a photo.

Unfortunately, people did not understand that we were only asking to have what we considered "extraordinary means" to be removed. We wanted our daughter returned to a natural state without the maze of technology. We wanted our daughter to be able to die a natural and peaceful death.

Overnight, Karen, as well as Joe and I, became what the press called *celebrities*, but not by choice. We never sought the glaring lights and the publicity.

In fact, we never allowed pictures of Karen to be taken. We would not allow her to become a spectacle. Our main objective from that point on, beyond protecting her right to die naturally, was to protect and preserve her dignity as a human being.

The papers at the time referred to Karen as the "Sleeping Beauty." Although we knew otherwise—that

Karen's physical condition was nothing like the glorified image of a "sleeping beauty"—we nevertheless wanted her to be remembered as such. No one needed to see what Karen really looked like.

Despite the constant media attention, we tried the best we could to go on with our lives—though our lives had changed dramatically. Our routines changed, and visiting our daughter through a maze of reporters every day soon became our way of life.

The Superior Court Decision

The weeks that we waited for a decision were extremely difficult. On November 10, 1975, Judge Muir reached his decision. Joe and I sat in the courtroom as the decision was read. It was not favorable. One by one, the superior court rejected each of the constitutional and religious arguments set forth by our attorney. The decision was even more devastating than we had expected. Judge Muir read the decision:

> Mr. Quinlan impresses me as a very sincere, moral, ethical and religious person. He very obviously anguished over his decision to terminate what he considers the extraordinary care of his daughter. That anguish would be continued and magnified by the inner conflicts he would have if he were required to concur in the day-by-day decision of the future of his daughter. I, therefore, find it appropriate and in Karen's interest if another guardian is appointed.

My heart ached for Joe. How could we have a stranger make life-and-death decisions for our daughter? All our decisions were made as a family out of love for Karen.

As we left the courthouse, we were faced with at least a hundred members of the media. They immediately started asking questions: "What are you going to do now?" one reporter called out. Joe could only reply, "We don't know what we're going to do now." He was visibly shaken and disappointed in the decision. The last thing we both wanted to do was face reporters and answer their questions.

"Do you intend to appeal?" another reporter asked. We needed time to think about it. We needed time to sit as a family and then make the decision whether or not to appeal to a higher court.

The next few days were difficult. We had questions that needed to be answered by one another. Would we each be able to tolerate the constant invasion of our privacy? Joe and I had protected Mary Ellen and John from reporters and the media as best we could up to that point, but could we continue to do so?

Mary Ellen and John listened intently to Joe and me and our feelings, and they shared their own as well. In the final analysis they both agreed: "Mom and Dad, there is no other decision but to appeal."

We then decided as a family that the best way we could help Karen was by appealing to the Supreme Court of New Jersey, the highest court in our state.

That evening I was very proud of my children. They set aside their fears and apprehensions out of love for their sister.

The Appeal

On November 17, 1975, our attorney filed an appeal with the appellate division of the New Jersey Supreme Court. The Supreme Court reacted promptly by announcing it would hear the case (thereby bypassing the intermediate appellate division) due to the important issues presented by the "tragic plight of Karen and the Quinlan family."

Hearing on the appeal was set for January 26, 1976.

I realized it was unusual for the Supreme Court to hear an appeal so quickly, so I was grateful for that decision. But the holidays were approaching, and I knew it would be a difficult time. Waiting for a decision only added to our stress. We knew memories of past celebrations would be with us.

I felt it important that we share the holidays together. My aging parents joined us for Thanksgiving dinner. After dinner we all visited Karen. It was very difficult for my mother and father, who were both in their eighties. They would always say, "It should be us lying there, not Karen. We lived our lives." They remained optimistic, however, that their grandchild would somehow recover. Perhaps that thought gave them the strength to carry on.

The next holiday would be more difficult. There were too many precious memories of Christmas that we shared as a family. As we attended Christmas Eve services, I thought of the time when Karen sang at Midnight Mass.

Memories are a gift. I felt very close to Karen that evening. She was with us in our prayers and the prayers of those present. Later, people came up to us to lend their support. Our Christian community was with us from day one. Prayer vigils were held for Karen and our family. It was a good feeling to know that we had their prayers and their support.

On Christmas day we visited Karen together and prayed together. We really didn't feel like celebrating and felt it would be best to have a quiet dinner in a restaurant. It was the first time and the last time we did that. That evening we agreed no matter how difficult it might be, holidays would be shared at home.

The New Jersey Supreme Court

Joe and I attended the Supreme Court hearing on January 26, 1976. We watched as history was being made. I tried to get a sense of how the judges would vote; but their questions were too diverse, and I could not get a sense of which way they were leaning.

The next two months would be a time of waiting and praying.

While awaiting the decision, we continued our way of life by visiting Karen every day and watching her struggle to release herself from the machine. She was losing weight (although she continued to receive nourishment through her nasal gastric feeding tube) and continued to stare straight ahead, never looking to the right or the left. She would be startled by the slightest sound.

How long will it be, how long? I pleaded with God.

When we received the news that a decision was reached, Joe, Father Tom and I traveled to Princeton and waited for the all-important call. It had been previously arranged that we would receive the call at the Nassau Inn in Princeton, New Jersey. When the phone rang, Father Tom answered it. "The decision was unanimous," he said. The court had appointed Joe guardian of our daughter. We just broke down, embraced and cried. It was an extremely emotional moment.

We were grateful to the court. Then reality set in and

we realized that Karen was going to die. Still, we were thankful that it would be a natural death and as peaceful as possible.

Later in the day we faced reporters and answered their many questions. Many of them had followed the case from the beginning. They sat in our living room, sometimes at the kitchen table. They had grown to know us and, I believe, respect us. They realized that we were sincere and that all the decisions we made were out of love for our daughter.

The New Jersey Supreme Court's unanimous decision on March 31, 1976, was based on an individual constitutional right of privacy: *Citizens could make decisions that profoundly affect their own lives.* The court concluded that Karen's right of privacy may be asserted on her behalf by her guardian under these peculiar circumstances. Even if the patient becomes incompetent because of accident or illness, that constitutionally protected right is not lost. It is transferred to those who know the patient best—her family, those who can best determine what the patient would decide if he or she were able.

The court was convinced of the "high character of Joseph Quinlan and his general suitability," describing him as "very sincere, moral, ethical and religious." The Supreme Court declared:

> Although Mr. Quinlan feels a natural grief, his strength of purpose and character far outweighs these sentiments and qualifies him eminently for guardianship of the person as well as the property of his daughter. [It is also concluded that] Karen's right of privacy be asserted on her behalf by her father. [Whatever he should decide to

do, regarding his daughter] should be accepted by society, the overwhelming majority of whose members, we think, in similar circumstances, would exercise such a choice in the same way for themselves or for those closest to them.

The court concluded that there would be no criminal homicide in the circumstances of this case. The decision also stated:

We believe, first, that the ensuing death would not be homicide but rather expiration from existing natural causes. Secondly, even if it were to be regarded as homicide, it would not be unlawful. The decision should be reviewed by a hospital Ethics Committee or like body of the institution in which Karen is then hospitalized.

The major newspapers grasped the significance of the issues. *The New Jersey Star Ledger* and *The New York Times* as well as other major papers printed the entire text of the Supreme Court decision. In retrospect, the media did a good job in educating the public about this otherwise taboo, but important, topic of death and dying.

Though the decision was in our favor and we had much to be happy about, Joe and I were still anxious to be with our daughter. We had no idea how or when the Supreme Court decision would be implemented. Also we did not know if St. Clare's Hospital would appeal. We had learned to take one day at a time and, above all, to be patient. When we left Karen on the evening of the appeal we wondered how much longer she would be with us. Although we wanted her to die peacefully, we were not ready to lose her.

Meanwhile, Mary Ellen and John had heard the news and were waiting for us at home. When Joe and I returned, we had very little to say. It was a quiet evening. What do you say to one another when you know you are going to lose someone you love?

The next day Joe and I returned to our jobs. Mary Ellen and John returned to their classes. We tried to go on with our lives in a normal way, but they were anything but.

We scheduled our days around our visits to Karen. There were days when she was terribly restless and looked like she was experiencing pain. We had little contact with the doctors and the hospital. After almost six weeks since the decision, no attempt had been made to start the weaning. Also they had not established an ethics committee, which was part of the decision. It appeared to me that they did not intend to comply with the decision.

Our attorney arranged a meeting with the hospital administration, their attorney and Karen's doctors. It was a most unpleasant meeting. Ultimately, St. Clare's refused to comply and carry out the court's decision.

Our relationship with Karen's doctors up until that point was deteriorating rapidly. They shunned us in the hallways. I doubt they realized the tremendous stress we were under. But after the meeting, Doctor Morse and Doctor Javed asked to speak to us privately. They said they would like to attempt to wean Karen off the respirator. I said a silent prayer of thanks.

The doctors assured us it would be slow, but safe process. Doctor Javed started the weaning on May 17, 1976. Joe and I spent day and night at the hospital. We both hoped that we would be with Karen should something happen.

By May 22 the weaning process was successfully completed. Karen appeared tired but peaceful. She no longer had to struggle to release herself from the respirator. I cannot put into words what a stressful week that was. We had no indication of how she would respond to the process. She could have died. We stayed at her beside for a very long time. Finally, we had to say goodnight and pray that she would be there for us tomorrow. We had no idea how long she would survive.

As soon as she was successfully weaned from the respirator, St. Clare's was pressing us to find another facility.

PART FIVE : A PLACE FOR KAREN

NOT QUITE DONE WITH ONE BATTLE, we had to fight another while trying to find a place that would welcome and care for our dying daughter.

It seemed that every facility in the state had its private reasons for not accepting my daughter. Twenty-two New Jersey institutions expressed sympathy and regret but found it impossible to accept her. The publicity involved undoubtedly affected their decision, but many facilities were not equipped to care for a comatose patient.

How I prayed that someone would open his or her doors to my daughter! By late May our attention had focused on Morris View Nursing Home, a spacious and modern institution operated by Morris County.

On June 3, 1976, in a secret and hastily called meeting by the board of Morris View Nursing Home, an ethics committee was formed in order to comply with the New Jersey Supreme Court decision. The board agreed that Karen Ann Quinlan would be treated with a "general medical and nursing care routine." It would be a relatively simple medical program. (Actually, their staff would administer less medication and care than they would offer many of the relatively healthy elderly patients.)

Morris View Nursing Home

Although Morris View Nursing agreed to take Karen, there was still the problem of Karen's security and privacy. Morris View is an open facility—with no secluded ends or private rooms. Anyone could access the patient halls from one end or the other, or even through the basement. Joe and I were concerned for Karen's safety. But again our prayers were answered when the Morris County Sheriff's office agreed to guard and secure Karen's room with armed deputies, twenty-four hours a day, for as long as she lived.

The Move

The move was scheduled for June 9, 1976. Absolute secrecy was essential in order to avoid a media frenzy. We decided that we couldn't use one of St. Clare's ambulances, because the media would be expecting that.

Our friend Father John Quinlan was captain of the Jefferson Township Volunteer Ambulance Squad, and he offered to provide the ambulance. We all thought that might throw off the press—seeing an ambulance from another town.

When we visited Karen that evening, she was quite calm. Her eyes were open, but she wasn't moving about and she wasn't grimacing. A nurse came into the room and said, "The press has been tipped off, Mrs. Quinlan. I think it would be best if you and Joe leave before Karen's ambulance arrives."

I leaned over and kissed my daughter. I realized then that it might be the last time I would see her alive. She was still critical and she hadn't been out of the hospital for nearly fourteen months. When two interns came hurrying toward her room with a stretcher, we knew Father Quinlan and his ambulance must be on the premises. We left Karen and drove to the nursing home to wait for her. How I wished I could have taken the ride with her.

Recognizing the security problems, Sheriff John Fox planned the move skillfully. There would be sixteen officers assigned to the transfer. Half of them posted at St. Clare's were to serve as guards and escorts during the twenty-minute drive to the nursing home. The other eight men were stationed inside and outside at Morris View to protect Karen on arrival.

I knew that Karen was on her way and that absolute secrecy was essential. Time moved very slowly as I waited. Finally, I saw the ambulance pull into the driveway. She was safe and I prayed that she was also still alive.

As we waited, we were not aware that there had been a threat on Karen's life. The sheriff had an armed guard placed inside the ambulance, along with a nurse, a doctor and a respiratory therapist. The sheriff drove his car in front of the ambulance and had another car follow behind it.

It was a hot, oppressive and hazy night with far-off flashes of lightning. The temperature lingered in the nineties even after the sun went down.

As the lightning drew closer, the sky burst into a torrential rain that was blinding as it beat against the windows. One flash of lightning was so powerful that it caused a blackout over the entire area.

This was a blessing. The blackout blinded the members of the media who were chasing the ambulance, hoping for a prized picture of the elusive "Sleeping Beauty," but it lasted only a few minutes. When the lights flashed back on, the huge doors to the entrance of the Morris View Nursing Home simultaneously swung open. At that exact moment Karen's stretcher, which had been hoisted from the back of the ambulance, was passed into the hands of sheriff's deputies. She was safely behind the doors before anyone could see her. Immediately, Karen's bed was wheeled into a waiting elevator and into her room.

Though Karen was finally safe and in a facility that would properly care for her, as a mother, I was still shaken by the events of that night. I had so much worry and anxiety. So many things could have gone wrong. *What if she died during the ambulance ride to the nursing home? What if someone broke through the police line? What if the doors didn't swing open? What if we didn't have such wonderful, caring friends that were willing to take a risk and bring Karen safely to the nursing home?*

Will Karen always be safe? What if someone tries to harm her?

My fears were relieved when I saw the guard placed at Karen's door. Morris View went to great lengths to ensure Karen's safety. They had a list of family members and close friends whom would be permitted to visit (since her accident and the subsequent court battles, there had been many intrusive attempts by the media, the curious and the zealously religious). The staff at Morris View sincerely cared for Karen and assured Joe and me that she would be safe.

The nurses gently lifted Karen's twisted body from the stretcher and placed her on a waterbed in a private room. The room was painted yellow and had a view of tall trees that she would never be able to see.

Karen looked like a small child, lying curled up in her big bed. A few days later, the nurses cut her hair short to make it easier for them to wash and dry. The media was not aware of this. Because of that now-famous graduation picture, the newspapers continued to refer to Karen as a "Sleeping Beauty" with beautiful, long hair. Though the hair, body and smile were gone, my daughter was still beautiful in my eyes. How I, too, wished she were only sleeping.

A whole series of heartrending events over a period of fourteen months reached a climax that evening:

- The terrible ordeal of having to accept a medical prognosis that dictated our beloved daughter would die.
- The indignation of watching her struggle against modern technology knowing it could not prolong her life—only her discomfort, her suffering and her eventual death.
- The awesome task of a family having to ask for the removal of an apparatus thought by most doctors to be the only thing keeping her alive.
- The perplexity of having the doctors and the hospital administration agree with our decision, only to have them change their minds two days later.
- The shock at being told that we did not have the right to make decisions for our helpless daughter.
- The determination to gain that right in court.

- The nightmare of a long trial.
- The pressure of meeting the press at all hours of the day and night.
- The frustration at the lower court's decision.
- The restlessness during the appeal process.
- The solution offered in the New Jersey Supreme Court decision.

I prayed that no other family would ever have to experience the same terrible ordeal to fight for a loved one.

It had been a long day for all of us and a stressful day for Karen. I kissed her goodnight and said, "I love you, and I will see you tomorrow." I knew she was exhausted and hoped she would have a restful night.

As I left, I thanked the guard that was placed at her door. For the first time in over a year, I felt the relief of knowing that she was safe and protected. I also thanked the nurses. They were very attentive to Karen and made her as comfortable as possible. As I shut her door, I shut the door on the first phase of our journey. I had no idea how long a journey it would be.

A New Way of Life for Us

Now that Karen was safe and receiving proper care, I knew I must reach out to my husband and children, to become a wife and mother again. For so long I had allowed them to live in Karen's shadow. I knew that tragedies tear many marriages apart, and I did not want that to happen to my family. Joe and I had always had a very close relationship, yet there were many days I doubted my marriage would survive and that our lives would ever return to "normal."

We were all under tremendous pressure. There were

days when I could not mention Karen's name at the dinner table, because John would leave the room. Only seventeen, he looked up to his big sister. There were days when I could not speak what was in my heart in Joe's presence; he was not ready to face the reality of Karen's ordeal. With his strong faith, he still thought that God would perform a miracle and bring his daughter back. Although it was Karen who was living and dying in a state of limbo, the rest of us were too in many, many ways.

As we drove home after Karen's arrival to Morris View, Joe and I spoke no words. Instead, we were both reliving our memories of Karen. I looked at my husband and wondered, *was he at peace?* It had been difficult for him to reach the decision to have Karen removed from the respirator. Yet at the trial he had put it beautifully: "I want my daughter to be placed back in a natural state without the maze of machinery, and allowed to die in God's time." As I looked at his face, I could see the toll the past year had taken on him—and on all of us.

I tried to read Mary Ellen and John's thoughts. I could not. This should have been a very happy time in their lives. Mary Ellen was a student at Centenary College in Hackettstown, and John had just graduated high school. Instead of experiencing some the most carefree times of their lives, they had to cope with not only the loss of their sister, but with the loss of their privacy. It was all but impossible for me to imagine how difficult it was for them.

A New Way of Life for Mary Ellen and John
Mary Ellen and John's lives were affected in many less obvious ways. Because Mary Ellen and John attended grade school and high school with their peers from the

same neighborhood, it was impossible to assume any sort of anonymity.

I remember when John asked his father if he could go to college out of state. In normal times this would not have been a problem, but we were not living in normal times. Joe and I were greatly concerned for John's security. We worried about him, and we did not want him to leave home. Nevertheless, we listened to John as he expressed his reasons. Mainly, he wanted to go someplace where his identity was not known. But after graduation he attended County College of Morris, as many of his friends did. People would stop him in the hall and ask about his sister—some had gone to school with Karen and were sincerely interested. Nevertheless, it was too much for any young person to bear. John needed to move on. Deciding whether or not to let John go away to college was a challenging decision for his father and I to make. We talked about it and prayed for guidance. The fears and the what-ifs were real. How could we let him go? But we had to overcome our fears, for there was only one question that mattered: "How could we *not* let him go?" He could not continue to live in his sister's shadow. Eventually, John did leave home. It was a positive experience. He grew in maturity and independence.

It was different for Mary Ellen. She was in her second year at college when Karen went into her coma. Centenary was a small, private college. Many of the students were from out of state. A few of the teachers were aware of who Mary Ellen was, but they respected her privacy. After graduation she continued her education at Loyola University in New Orleans, obtaining a master's degree.

When she left for Loyola, she and I drove down in her Pinto. Her father joined us later, and I flew home with him. It was quite an experience for mother and daughter. We drove for over twenty hours, making very few stops. We snacked on chips and pretzels. We talked and shared memories and many laughs. When we arrived in New Orleans, our first task was to find her a place to live. We rented a small studio apartment right on St. Charles Avenue.

Mary Ellen was excited and apprehensive; this was a university she would be attending, not a small college. However, she had no problem adjusting to her new life. She enjoyed the two years she spent there and developed many new friendships. It also gave her the opportunity to grow in maturity and independence.

All in all, Mary Ellen and John adjusted to their new lives beautifully. In time Joe and I did, too.

A New Way of Life for Karen

Meanwhile Karen, too, had moved on in a way. Her new home in Morris View was a major—and a good—change for all of us.

The last several months that Karen was a patient at St. Clare's were extremely stressful for Joe and me. Because of the New Jersey Supreme Court decision and the hospital's reluctance to abide by the decision, we had little contact with her doctor. He avoided us whenever possible until one day when he approached Joe and me in the hallway. He asked that we stop our daily visits, since they were upsetting the nurses. His statement outraged us. I felt it was inappropriate and insensitive. Didn't he realize that our daughter was dying and we wanted to spend every possible moment we could with her? Of course we ignored the doctor's suggestion, continued our visits and had no further contact with him.

However, at Morris View we found the staff had the opposite philosophy about Karen's care. The nurses encouraged us to talk constantly to her and to play the radio in her room. A few of her friends continued to visit, hopeful they might get a response. The nurses talked to Karen when they bathed her and changed her bedding. Doctor Wolf, Karen's doctor, was always available to us. He answered many questions and supported us. He and the nurses treated her as she was, a living person—not for her sake only, but for all of us.

I brought pretty nightgowns for her. It was a joy to wash and press them. As I stood by her bedside and placed my hands around her twisted fingers, I could only thank God that now I could hold her and get close enough to kiss her, without a cage of machinery surrounding her. The quiet time I spent at her bedside was a time of prayer and reflection.

Visiting our daughter every day continued to be our way of life. Joe would visit every morning before going to the office and every evening before coming home. I visited every afternoon. I don't know how often Mary Ellen and John visited their sister. It's hard to express, but this was a very private time even within the family. We each had our own memories to share with Karen.

A few days after she was admitted to the nursing home, Karen developed pneumonia. Her doctors felt she would not survive in her weakened condition. Maintaining a vigil at her bedside throughout the night, I was able to observe the treatment she received. The doctor and nurses were constantly in her room. I was struck by their calm, professional demeanor and deep concern for my daughter.

The quality of the life Karen had was important to them. They treated her with the dignity any human being deserves—whether or not that human being has the cognitive awareness to appreciate that care. They showed me the worth of caring for someone beyond curing.

This was the first of Karen's many episodes of high fever, infections and bouts of pneumonia. Each time I thought it would be her last. But Karen was a strong, young woman. For some reason she kept fighting back. I felt like she was saying, "It is not time, Mom."

I prayed every day that I'd be with her when the time came.

I remember a day in August when I visited Karen. She was so peaceful that I wanted to stay longer. On the drive home I kept thinking about her, as I usually did. I'd remember some foolish or silly thing she did, like lifting me up and swinging me around laughing. Then we would both laugh. She loved life, loved people and loved helping her friends. Then there were many times when I don't know how I made it home driving through the tears. So much depended on how her mood had seemed. Was it a good day or a restless day? This particular day it had been good.

In the middle of that night, the phone rang. It was Karen's nurse "Mrs. Quinlan, Karen is having a problem breathing. I suggest you and your husband come immediately." We both dressed quickly and rushed out of the house. When we entered her room, the nurse was with her.

Her bedding had been changed and her hair washed. She was wearing a fresh nightgown and looked very peaceful. The nurse said, "She had a mucous blockage in her throat, but we were able to clear it up by a routine procedure." It turned out to be a non-threatening episode. We were relieved and thankful that they called us.

We stayed with Karen until we felt the danger had passed. As I kissed her good night, I wondered if she had felt any pain. I told her I loved her and wondered if she heard me, maybe just this once. I knew the answer, but sometimes your heart, not your intellect, rules you.

We continued our daily visits. Once or twice a week I brought my parents to visit Karen. It was difficult for them to accept what had happened. Karen was so much a part of their lives. She would bring her friends to visit grandma and grandpa. Sometimes she would take them for a ride in her little green Bug. She enjoyed their company and, of course, they relished the extra-special attention.

During their visits to the hospital, I stood back and watched them rub Karen's head or her arms. Mama would always say, "Hurry up and get better, Karen." Papa would always repeat it.

It was heartbreaking to watch, yet beautiful and tender.

The love she shared with her grandparents was special. On the ride home they would talk about all the little things that Karen used to do for them and how much they missed her visits. I never allowed them to see their granddaughter beyond her arms and neck. Knowing the terrible toll Karen's condition had taken on her body, it would serve no purpose and it could have had a devastating effect on them. Karen was still the same beautiful Karen in their eyes. I wanted them to remember her that way.

Christmas 1977

The days and the months passed slowly. Another spring, another summer and soon the holiday season was approaching. Christmas had always been a special holiday for us. We had always attended Midnight Mass as a family. When we returned home, we would open a few gifts and save the big ones for Christmas Day.

Early that Christmas week, I had placed a manger in Karen's room—it was part of our tradition. I was thankful that we were all able to share one more holiday together. On Christmas Day, as I often did while I sat with Karen, I wrote poetry. It was my way of expressing my feelings. Once again I was mindful that the end could happen at any time. Of all my poems, this one is most special to me:

Christmas 1977

> As I sit at her bedside
> this Christmas Day
> My thoughts turn to Christmas
> of '54.
> A house filled
> with love, laughter and toys
> Did I thank you then, Lord
> for the birth of our child?
> For her beautiful face,
> radiating love throughout our house.
> For the cleft in her chin,
> for her dancing blue eyes.
> Did I thank you then, Lord
> for Christmas of '55?

The toddler, awed by the glimmer
of tree lights, shimmering tinsel,
white snow and ice.
Did I thank you then, Lord,
for Christmas of '57?
Three precious angels
gathered 'round the tree—
our gifts from heaven.
Did I thank you, Lord,
for each Christmas that followed?
For your love. For your gifts.
For the joys and the laughter.
Did I thank you then, Lord,
for the Christmas of '75?
When our lights
were dimmed.
No dancing blue eyes.
As I sit by her bedside today,
my heart is filled with love
for my beautiful child.
I thank you, Lord,
for this Christmas Day.
For now I am able to see
beyond the Christmas trees,
the holly wreaths, and Santa Claus.
For now I see the true meaning of Christmas:
The birth of a child,
the sacredness of life,
the joys of sorrow.
I see Love.
I see Christ.

PART SIX : "IN THE MATTER OF KAREN ANN QUINLAN"

As the interest in Karen's life-and-death situation grew in 1975 and on into early 1976—not just on the nightly news or in the daily newspapers, but in magazines and talk shows—Joe and I were faced with another question, who would we rather have tell our story? The media or us? To be honest, Joe and I were not sure we wanted to share memories of Karen and our family with the world. So much was written about our daughter. They wrote about Karen and the night she went into the coma, the Supreme Court's landmark decision and the impact it had on healthcare decisions. They wrote about the right we all have to make decisions about our lives and our loved ones should he or she be incapacitated. We knew it was an important story, that it was part of our history and that Karen's life was a constant reminder of the importance of these issues, but Karen was still just our daughter—my other two children's sister. It was hard to see her as anything else but that.

After many, many family discussions, we did feel compelled to tell our version of the story. We felt strongly that no one else could write about the profound pain and anguish that we felt. We were living then with the results of our decisions and knew we would have to live with them for the rest of our lives. Others may have written about it, but they did not live it.

There were a lot of rumors and conjecture at the time, and as I said previously, not all the articles written about Karen—or us—were favorable. Joe and I felt very strongly that we wanted the truth to be told. But we also felt equally strong about another point: we did not want to make any money from Karen's suffering. So Joe and I made a vow: *We would not use any of the money we made from Karen's story for our own purposes.* Instead, we agreed that we would use any money earned to benefit others in similar situations, although at the time we had no idea what the charity would be. Until we found a suitable charity, we established a special foundation to accept the donations or money we received.

The Book

Once we decided we were ready to share our story, we needed to find someone to help us write it. Neither Joe nor I were experienced writers. In fact, we had no knowledge of the publishing world at all. But in early 1976 a representative from *Ladies' Home Journal* arranged for us to interview different writers that might be interested in the story. It was important for us to find the right person. We had to work closely with that person and let that person into our family. After interviewing a number of writers with whom we did not feel comfortable, someone at

Ladies' Home Journal suggested we meet with Phyllis Battelle. Just minutes into our conversation we were relaxed enough to begin sharing some of our feelings. Phyllis was low-key and perceptive. She listened to our thoughts and our fears with sensitivity. With her gentle manner she was capable of drawing out important information. I was particularly impressed with the way Joe was able to express his love and anger, though I was very surprised that he shared these emotions with her. He rarely talked about these feelings—even with me.

Once we chose Phyllis, we knew we would have to take her to see Karen. We knew the entire story could not be told without Phyllis seeing Karen's condition for herself. We requested only that no photographs be taken, and that, of course, she treat Karen as living, breathing human being with rights and dignity.

Phyllis Battelle was the only member of the press ever to visit Karen. Below is her response to seeing Karen for the first time.

I first visited Karen in the evening of May 17, 1976, in the intensive care unit of St. Clare's Hospital. My reaction was not shock or revulsion but deep pity, a feeling of "Oh, the poor child." She looked like a child. Her body was a small, rounded mold concealed under a sheet. All that was exposed were head and her hands. The hands were drawn tight over the chest.

In later visits at the Morris View Nursing Home, I saw Karen's body free of the masking sheet. It was emaciated, and seemed totally foreign to the round and still attractive (even when contorted) face.

For me, watching her face has been an emotional,

rather than a rational experience. When her face is composed, it is easy to slip into the illogical rationale that Karen is a "sleeping beauty" as some of the media have imagined. (*Karen Ann*, Doubleday & Co., 1977)

Ultimately, Phyllis was able to help Joe and I capture the depth of the love we had for Karen and the deep love we shared as a family in the book *Karen Ann*. The book was taut, absorbing and moving. I was very pleased with the result. It proved to be a great success, and the interest in our case was so phenomenal that it was translated and published in both Spanish and Japanese.

For me, and I think also for Joe, it was an awesome feeling to walk into a bookstore and stare at a picture of Karen. It was a feeling I never grew accustomed to. But I realized then, as I do now, Karen's life was not to be cherished by us alone; she was loved and embraced by the entire world. Though we never wished to be celebrities or to have our daughter's picture on the cover of a book jacket, I was pleased that finally we had the opportunity to turn this tragedy into something good.

The Movie

One cold rainy evening in 1977, Joe and I met the producer and writer for the television movie, *In the Matter of Karen Ann Quinlan* at Newark airport. It wasn't difficult to identify them. They were the two shivering passengers dressed for Los Angeles weather.

They came to New Jersey to finalize the production of the movie. The following three days we went over the script and made changes. We were assured the movie would not be sensationalized, but it would be a serious drama based on fact. The focus of the movie was to be on the family, and how we made the decisions we did. We asked that there be no "re-creations" or pictures of Karen in her hospital bed. The producers complied and instead only filmed us (actually, the actor and actress that played us) standing at Karen's bedside.

The movie recounted the mental anguish and spiritual suffering of our family during the court hearings. It re-created the battle which pitted us against legal and medical experts who argued that there was a compelling state interest to preserve life. It also conveyed the central place of our faith as we tried to put into action our Christian ethics.

Brian Keith was chosen to play Joe. One evening I answered the phone and an unfamiliar voice said, "Hello, this is Brian Keith. May I speak to Joe Quinlan?" I handed the phone to my husband; he was not at all intimidated.

"Hello, Brian, this is Joe. I hear you will play the role of Karen's father in the movie."

Brian had then said he wanted to talk to Joe to get a feel for his emotions and the type of man he was. They talked for a while. And soon they discovered there were many parallels in their lives. They practically grew up neighbors. Brian was from Jersey City, and Joe was from the next town, Union City. Brian said he never really lost his accent and neither had Joe. Also, they were about the same age. They talked about changes in Jersey City, in the area they grew up in, and they touched on their service in the military. After that phone conversation Brian Keith was not just one of my husband's favorite actors, he was the only favorite.

Just as Joe was pleased with the actor who played him, I was pleased Piper Laurie was chosen to play my part. She was not only a fine actress, but also petite in stature (like me). Piper Laurie was very effective, subtle and restrained. As John J. O'Connor from *The New York Times* said, "using intelligent understatements, she [Piper Laurie] dominates everyone and everything around her" (September 26, 1977). Similarly, Brian Keith created a character of an almost awkward, but utterly convincing goodness. He was able to capture Joe's speech, manner and the quiet intensity of his feelings.

As a family we watched the movie with a small group of friends at Our Lady of the Lake rectory. It was difficult to watch, sometimes recalling too sharply the events that happened. Seeing the dramatization version of my family's long ordeal was like reliving it all over again. There were some inaccuracies, but overall we were pleased with it. It remained generally true to the facts.

The Letters Pour In

After the publication of the book and the television movie, letters once again began to flood our home and the nursing home. The story touched the lives of many ordinary people. Parents across the country saw our family as being similar to their own. They saw our tragedy as something which could easily happen in their own homes. It was easy for a brother or a sister to relate to Karen. People realized it could happen to them. We received letter after letter from families who wanted to share their heartache of caring for a relative or who had lost a loved one. I was then, as I am now, genuinely touched by the sincerity of so many strangers. I'll never know the number of lives that were affected by our fight for Karen's wishes.

Public Opinion

Fortunately for me, my husband made a scrapbook of every newspaper and magazine article covering the story. He did not discriminate; favorable and unfavorable articles were placed in the book. It was a tremendous help to me in my research. In reading the stories once again, it refreshed my memory of things that happened thirty years ago, some that I had put out of my mind.

Our case had become synonymous with the phrase "the right to die." Our privacy had been totally erased. We had been inundated with the media and reporters. The case was the lead story on the network channels for the six o'clock news. The interest in the case was phenomenal. Nearly every day a story about Karen, the case or our family appeared in the local and international newspapers. But we realized the importance of informing the public of exactly what we had requested of the courts.

Prior to our case there was little or no discussion on this particular issue. However, all that changed when we went to court to fight for what we believed in and what we knew were Karen's wishes. We were fighting for the right to remove an artificial life-support system that offered no hope of success. A way of life was chosen. Death was not desired, only accepted. We felt that to choose *not to prolong life artificially* was the ultimate respect for human life. We did not see it as murder or genocide as others suggested it was.

In retrospect, I understand why so many people had difficulty with our decision. We were at crossroads in society—our technology was such that it could sustain life indefinitely, but we had no means to measure or to decide if the quality of life warranted life-saving procedures. We could prolong life, but we could not make that life better. No, we could not heal or cure a person surviving only by machines. We could only prolong a person's dying. Our society, in its fear and denial of death, was hanging onto life for as long as it possibly could. Today we take it for granted that we have such things as living wills, in which we can choose in advance if we want extraordinary means to be taken to save or continue our own lives. We also are fully aware of our rights now, thanks to Karen's case. Although many of our societal norms are not completely different, we have at least become more sensitive to the notion of dying with dignity—particularly the forms of hospice care, counseling and bereavement services. In the late 1970s these notions and/or services were in the infant stage of development.

As I reread the stories, I looked at them from a different perspective. During those difficult years there were times when I found the media and the press unbearable. In retrospect, I realize they had a job to do. The media was a positive tool in educating the public about the issues. They all did a wonderful job. Sure there were those in television and newspapers who searched for the sensational and who filled their stories with innuendo, but they were in the minority. At the time their stories hurt my family deeply. But whatever they wrote could never change our memories of Karen. As time passed, I forgot the cruel or fictitious stories, and I remembered only the true ones.

After the Supreme Court decision papers like *The New*

Jersey Star Ledger and *The New York Times* printed the entire text of the decision. They realized the importance of the issues and that they were writing history. As I read and reread the decision, I was touched by the sensitivity and importance they placed on the family. *Who best would know the wishes of their loved one?* They also emphasized the decision-making process and the right we have as patients to accept or refuse treatment—and ultimately—that we do not lose this right when we are incapacitated. This was unheard of before 1975.

College students across the country were asked their feelings on the prolonging of life. Discussions were held in schools. The topics of numerous conferences held throughout the nation were death with dignity and the right to die.

Soon it became clear to me that Joe and I were not alone. Many parents—many people, rather—felt the way we did. So often (too often) I heard the claim, "I don't want to be another Karen Ann Quinlan."

During Karen's ordeal *Ladies' Home Journal* conducted a poll. They asked several questions related to end-of-life issues.

How do women feel about treating the terminally ill? Do human beings have the right to decide life-or-death for other human beings? The recent Karen Ann Quinlan case, in which the parents of a comatose girl have fought to turn off her life-supporting machines, has highlighted the ethical and religious aspects of the "pull the plug" decision, and we decided to ask American women how they felt.

A majority of women polled in a 16-city survey of both *Journal* and non-*Journal* readers, overwhelmingly agree with the Quinlans' decision to fight to let their daughter die. And the women's opinions about other life-and-death subjects were equally interesting.

The *Journal's* poll revealed that three out of four women who had an opinion agreed the Quinlans' should have fought to have the machines turned off. Of all the women questioned…60 percent said the machines should be turned off, 20 percent favored continuation, and the remaining 20 percent had no opinion.

We asked the women what they would do if one of their loved ones was terminally ill, without hope for survival, but was being kept alive by machines. More than 80 percent of those expressing an opinion opted for turning off the machines…showing a 9 percent increase in approval when the situation became personal. …

Suppose, we said, you were the terminally ill patient. What would you do? A staggering 86 percent of women making the choice said they'd want the machines discontinued. (*Ladies' Homes Journal*, "Pulling the Plug…Is It Murder or Mercy?" March 1976, pp. 98–99)

Articles like this encouraged Joe and me. We no longer felt alone or ostracized for our beliefs. We felt that we were right in our decisions and that Karen's life and dying were serving a purpose—a purpose others would benefit from—in 1977 and beyond.

PART SEVEN : THE KAREN ANN QUINLAN HOSPICE

IN 1977, WHILE WE WERE WORKING on the book and movie and keeping watch over Karen, Joe and I also began our search to establish a charity in Karen's name.

When Karen was in the intensive care unit at St. Clare's, I became acutely aware of the needs of a dying person. Because of the tangle of machines that were attached to her, I was unable to get close enough to kiss her or to hold her.

I also had the opportunity to observe the frustrations and anxieties of other patients' families. At that time families were only permitted to visit for five minutes on the half-hour. I felt the environment and atmosphere were not conducive to the needs of dying persons and their families. This was the time a family wanted to be near their loved one and to spend as many precious moments together as possible. The family should be free to express themselves and to communicate in a loving way.

Thankfully, many changes have occurred in ICUs since

1975, and it is an entirely different environment today—there is a better understanding of patient and family needs.

When Karen was transferred to the nursing home, I had the opportunity to see the importance of caring for a patient that was beyond curing. I watched them gently bathe my daughter and talk to her as they turned her body. They treated her in a most compassionate way. It was then I realized that loving support is more important than mechanical support. In my heart I felt there must be a more humane way to care for the dying.

Death and long-term dependencies are negatives. Our hope was to turn our thoughts and energies into a positive action. As a result of our tragedy, we made the decision to dedicate ourselves to establishing a program that would help families in similar situations. Finally, we had found a way in which we could use the funds from Karen Ann's foundation.

When I read about a new program called hospice that offered both medical and physical care, as well as emotional and spiritual support to terminally ill patients and their families, I knew I had to learn more about it. In my study I found that the hospice care was usually given in the comfortable and familiar surroundings of a patient's home. Immediately, I knew I had to become a part of the hospice movement—for Karen's sake and for her lasting memory.

The Greeks were thought to have originated the concept of a place to go to die before 1000 B.C. In medieval times a hospice was a way station associated with a religious order. The movement has its modern roots in a home for the dying opened in Dublin, Ireland, in the late nineteenth century by an associate of Florence Nightingale.

Not much later, the Sisters of Charity opened a similar home in London, England. It was largely at that home in the 1950s and the 1960s that Dame Cicely Saunders developed her idea for a modern hospice that would bring physical and spiritual peace in the face of death.

Elisabeth Kübler-Ross launched the hospice movement in the United States in the 1970s and 1980s. In her landmark book *On Death and Dying*, she lambasted the medical community for its lack of compassion and its inability to care appropriately for the dying patient.

The book cites many examples of neglected individuals who experienced excruciating pain, while being exhorted to be quiet and not complain. It encouraged a movement dedicated to the mission of serving the dying.

Out of this cultural backdrop, hospice was born. The first hospice began in Connecticut in 1975. Since then more than 2,500 hospices have come into existence.

For three years my husband and I made a study of hospices and hospice-type facilities in our area and bordering states. We visited Mother Cabrini Hospice, Rose of Hawthorne and Calgary Hospital in New York. We traveled to the West coast and met with Elisabeth Kübler-Ross personally. Then we traveled on to Arizona to visit a hospice that was connected with a hospital and a nursing home. We also traveled to London and had the privilege to meet Dame Cicely Saunders.

There was joy and laughter in these facilities. I did not sense a fear of death, only an acceptance. Most of the hospices we visited were institutions. Cicely Saunders advised us to visit the Hospice of Marin in Marin County, California, where they have a home-care program. We met with their founder and medical director, Doctor William Lamers. He explained how they treated the patient and the family as a unit. He told us about the extensive training program they have for their patient care volunteers. We met their staff and a few volunteers. It was all very encouraging.

When I returned home I took the volunteer patient care training course at Riverside Hospice in Boonton, New Jersey. It was an in-care facility with only a few beds. There was a living room, dining room and kitchen all in a very homelike setting. Trees and flowers surrounded its lovely patio. It was a very peaceful setting for those experiencing their last days. At the conclusion of my training, I was assigned a patient.

One of my patients was a wonderful elderly man named John. He had cancer of the throat and was unable to speak. I would hold his hand while I read his favorite poetry. It was a beautiful experience. I was there to bring some joy into his life, but I came away with more than I gave.

A trust and everlasting friendship grew among John, his wife and me. When he died, I felt I had lost a dear friend.

After almost three years of searching, praying and planning as a family, we made the decision to establish a hospice in Karen's name. Although she could not benefit from hospice, I felt in some ways she symbolized one of the most difficult issues of our time—the treatment of the terminally ill. She had come to symbolize the difficulty some have dying in this age of eternal life.

We formed a core group to brainstorm different ideas. How do we start? Where would we establish the hospice?

What kind of program did we want? We had many questions and we needed to search for the answers. Step one was to conduct a feasibility study. There was an established hospice in Morris County and there was no need for a second one. We were unfamiliar with neighboring Sussex County, but a member of the core group lived there and was able to introduce us to the right people.

An informal meeting was held at Newton Memorial Hospital. The hospital administrator, doctors, health care providers and residents attended. I explained to them the reason for establishing the hospice in Karen's name. I told them about the different hospices Joe and I had visited across the country. They were interested and asked many questions about this new concept of care. The hospital administrators were most gracious and offered us space in the hospital. It was a very positive meeting. We even set a date for the opening, which was to be held in the conference room of the hospital.

The risks in establishing our hospice were enormous, financially and emotionally. There were no guarantees for success. We only had the money from the sale of our book to use. We never received government funding, and Medicare did not recognize hospice at that time. It was a new concept of care we were offering to the people of this rural county.

We started with one paid staff member, an administrator. We hired nurses per diem and used volunteers for office work. In the beginning we cared for three or four patients a day. Gradually the program started to grow. Eventually, we held our first training class and hired a full-time nurse. We were on our way.

Exactly five years from the day that Karen was admitted to Newton Memorial Hospital, the opening ceremony was held. It was an overwhelming moment—somewhat solemn, somewhat nervous, and mostly hopeful—for me to return to where it all started. I wasn't sure I could handle it. The conference room was filled with reporters, television crews, family, friends and members of the community. Monsignor Thomas Trapasso opened the ceremony with a prayer. Then it was my turn to speak.

> Today, April 15, 1980, the Karen Ann Quinlan Center of Hope Hospice had its official opening. Today I have the joy and the sorrow of knowing that through my daughter's tragedy something beautiful has resulted.
>
> I cannot help but reflect on the past five years. I realize that Karen's life has a purpose far beyond what she or we could have suspected, certainly far beyond my expectations.
>
> So many thoughts and memories are rushing through my mind. Some time hopefully will erase; some I will cherish for life: the memory of her great energy, love of sports and her sense of humor. And her beautiful smile is as much with me today as it was before everything happened.
>
> Also, in reflecting on the past, I realize that my family and I have much to be thankful for. Somehow, through God's help we crossed a threshold into a world where life has a deeper meaning.
>
> I am so grateful that as a family we had the strength and the courage to fight for what we believed in and to turn the most traumatic experience of our lives into something positive for the people of Sussex County.

I thank you for the warm welcome you extend to us today. Hospice is a new concept of health and with your support we will be able to reach out to the patients and families that will be in need of our services.

Thank you for this memorable day.

It was quite an emotional day for me. I was overcome with tears of joy.

On that day, and in the years building up to that day, hospice had become an important part of my life. It was, unbeknownst to me then, to become my life's dedication.

PART EIGHT : KAREN CONTINUES TO FIGHT

EARLY ONE MORNING IN JUNE 1979, once again the dreaded phone call came in the middle of the night. Karen was experiencing difficulty. Joe, the children and I rushed to her side and maintained a vigil through the night. Her condition had weakened, and we thought it might be the end of her struggle. I called my dear friend Monsignor Trapasso. He came immediately and administered the sacrament of anointing of the sick. He had done this several times in the past.

Complying with guidelines established by the New Jersey Supreme Court and the Morris View ethics committee, our family and Doctor Wolf decided that no "heroic" measures would be taken.

We waited and prayed. Once again I witnessed the loving care the nurses gave Karen. I wiped the sweat from her face, dried her hair and waited. She had a high temperature. After two long days she weathered the crisis. Her condition stabilized. Joe returned to work. Mary Ellen and

John returned to their classes. I maintained my vigil at her bedside. I sat quietly wondering when would the next crisis occur. I questioned myself. Was I prepared for her death?

Though we had purchased a family plot in Gate of Heaven Cemetery and made all the necessary arrangements, I still pondered the question, and I knew I wasn't ready. I doubted that I could ever be totally prepared for the end. I felt helpless sitting there, but I could not leave. I had no profound thoughts. I only I wanted to be in her presence.

So did everyone else, it seemed.

Trying to Heal (Spare) Karen

Over the years, as each crisis occurred, the press was there waiting and maintaining a death watch, sometimes throughout the night. They would not leave until the last member of my family left. There were often television and radio technicians and curious onlookers waiting to hear any shred of news.

They were not all waiting for Karen to die; some were praying for a miracle. Some were just praying for our family. A Cherokee Native American tried to get into the nursing home, because he believed he could heal Karen. Faith healers claimed they were sent by the Lord to transmit the miracle that would heal Karen.

One said she was the vessel that Jesus uses to heal through. She and her two disciples wanted to pray over Karen. When they were unable to enter the nursing home, they prayed over a letter they wrote that was then given to a nursing home worker to give to us.

Even a Catholic group held a prayer group on the grounds. About eighty or more members of the group arrived unannounced with signs, flags and banners. They prayed on the grounds for two hours. They asked permission to take a picture of Karen. They were convinced they could cure my daughter and that we were wrong in letting her die.

The group did not cause any trouble, but additional sheriff's officers were called to the scene. The additional manpower, said Sheriff Fox, was a precaution, and the officers were sent home after the prayer vigil ended.

A delegation from the Manhattan-based Church of Humanism presented a petition asking that Karen be given "psychological, psychedelic and other alternate medical measures." Church of Humanism workers hoped to distribute "Get Karen Out of Coma" literature on the Morristown Green in Morristown, New Jersey.

Meanwhile, another group claimed the state Supreme Court's decision was "tantamount to murder with immunity."

Over the years we became somewhat accustomed to the fringe groups, and we learned to tune out the negative and hurtful words. We knew that although most people's intentions were good, they were not necessarily working in Karen's or our family's best interest.

However, some attempts to contact, "spare" or save Karen were just downright ludicrous.

For example, on the day following Karen's ordeal in June of 1979, a bomb threat was reported to the nursing home. A caller said he represented the "Right to Die Organization" and that dynamite would explode at the hospital at 4:15 P.M. The Morris County Sheriff's office, Morris Township police and the Morris Township fire department were called in and immediately conducted a search. Thankfully, the search failed to turn up any explosives.

Protecting Karen
Because of the expense of the sheriff's guard, we installed a special door with an electronic lock and burglar system in her room. The new lock and alarm were wired to a nursing station down the hall from Karen's room. My family, nurses and close friends held keys. Any attempts to enter the room without the passkey would trigger a series of alarm sounds and flashing lights on the floor. The sheriff's men would be notified and could arrive in a matter of minutes.

There were many past incidents of people trying to enter the room. One was a television reporter dressed as a nun. Faith healers and the curious made many attempts. None were successful due to the vigilance of the nurses and the sheriff's department. Sheriff Fox and his men did a thorough job of protecting Karen from day one to the very end.

A reporter attempted to buy detailed information about Karen's medical care from an employee of Morris View. Two employees were approached in the parking lot of Morris View and were offered three hundred to four hundred dollars each for information. Thankfully, they reported the incident. The sheriff's office was able to trace the reporter's license plate number, which one of the employees copied. It was traced to a Florida-based paper.

Another reporter from a weekly paper approached me. He offered me one hundred thousand dollars for a picture of Karen in her bed at the nursing home. I was so shaken

I couldn't answer him. He misread my silence and said, "That was only a starting figure." I rolled up my car window and sped away—still shaking.

I continued my daily visits. I'd read the nurses' notes to see what kind of a night Karen had. Was she restless? How often was she suctioned? Sometimes when I visited she was sweating; her hair would be wet and curly. It reminded me of when she was a small child. Like mothers with small children, if Karen had a bad night, it affected me for the rest of the day.

One day a reporter approached me and asked, "Why do you visit?" I thought that a strange question. How could I not visit? How could I not say goodnight to my daughter every night?

PART NINE : LIFE CHANGES

FOR THE NEXT FOUR YEARS WE EXPERIENCED many highs and lows. We were never quite certain when Karen's time would come. Although they were very anxious years, they were also years filled with exhilaration and a newfound purpose—especially with the opening of the hospice in 1980. Despite Karen's condition, Joe and I tried the best we could to maintain a semblance of normalcy.

The Move to Sussex County
In 1983 we made the decision to move to Sussex County, New Jersey. We had lived in the house in Landing for thirty-one years. It was the only home our three children knew. Now our lives had changed—they had changed in so many ways since that fateful day in 1975—and we were ready to move on.

Mary Ellen had graduated from Loyola and was doing her internship at a psychiatric hospital in Pennsylvania. John had his own business and was living in Elizabeth, New Jersey. Joe and I were living in the house alone with our memories, and at times those memories were too much to bear.

We felt that living in Sussex County, where our hospice was located, would give us the opportunity to become more involved and aware of the impact the hospice we established was having on the families and the communities we served.

Our house was sold before we put it on the market. On the day of the closing, Joe and I walked the property for the last time. I could see the three children playing in the yard. I could see us all gathered round the beautiful brick barbeque Joe had built complete with a sink, electricity and a rotisserie. I relived all the birthday celebrations, First Communions, confirmations, graduations and pajama parties. While Joe finished packing the truck, I walked through the empty rooms alone with my memories. I walked the property alone, taking one last look. When I locked the door and said my good-byes, I locked all those memories in my heart. As we drove away, I never looked back and I have never returned. That part of my life was over, the memories will stay with me always.

We rented a house in Sussex County while we familiarized ourselves with the area and searched for land on which to build our future home. My parents were quite elderly (my mother was ninety and my father was ninety-two), and we invited them to live with us. We had always enjoyed a close relationship and now we were given the opportunity to make whatever remaining years they had left as carefree and happy as possible. They were both alert and capable of making their own decisions, but I didn't feel comfortable leaving them on their own.

Another Accident

One beautiful day in March 1983, friends from Landing were on their way to visit Joe and me. I had had a very busy day and I was late coming home and late to prepare dinner—*it was just one of those days.* Then I realized I had nothing special to offer my friends. The cupboards were bare of cakes and cookies. After dinner I said, "I'm going to Shop-Rite to pick up a few goodies for this evening. I won't be long." My father asked if he could come. I said, "Not tonight. I'm in a bit of a hurry. I'm only going to pick up a few items and then head for home."

As I was driving south on Route 23, I hit black ice. I was driving our new truck and slid across the highway into a thirty-foot-high stonewall. That was the last thing I remembered. I would not recall what happened that evening for many, many months. I had completely blocked it out of my mind. Later I would learn that a state trooper had traveled that road minutes before me. He informed the road crew about the black ice; they were on their way to fix it. I also learned later that this section of the highway was one of the most dangerous and the first to freeze. Knowledge learned a little too late.

Meanwhile, my friends were on their way to visit me. In fact, they drove right past me. As they passed the truck, one remarked, "Look at that truck, it hit a concrete wall and crumbled. I doubt there are any survivors."

When they reached my home, they found Joe pacing back and forth in front of the house. When Joe saw them, he said, "I don't know where Julia is. She went to the store and hasn't returned. She's driving our new truck."

Panic-stricken, my friends realized it was my truck they had passed. They remembered thinking no one could have survived. They wondered *how do we tell Joe? How can we soften the blow?* They told Joe they had passed a truck that had been in an accident and suggested he call the local hospital. He did, and they confirmed that it was indeed me who had been in the accident. They told him a woman had been brought in earlier, and that she was alive.

My friend Maureen drove Joe to the hospital, knowing that they would pass the scene of the accident. There was no other route to take. Later he told me that after seeing the truck, he feared going into the ICU. He didn't know what condition I would be in.

I was awake and able to talk to him, but I had a triple concussion. When I looked at Joe, I saw three of him. When I looked up at the ceiling light there were three. Everything was in triplicate. My right leg was broken in several places, as was my right arm. I had multiple contusions to my chest. My head hurt, my chest hurt and I ached all over, but I was alive. I had been wearing my seat belt. It probably saved my life.

Maureen called my other friends, Anita and Terry, who were at the house. She related all the details and asked them to call Mary Ellen and John. They told my parents that I had an accident but that I was all right. They stayed with my parents until Joe came home. It had to have been a frightful night for all.

Much later, when I was able to organize my thoughts, I was so thankful that I did not take my father with me. He almost certainly would have been killed. I'm not sure I could have lived with that responsibility.

The cast on my leg extended from my ankle to my thigh. It was removed after eight months. Then I began extensive physical therapy for my injured leg and arm. I had the most wonderful therapist—I loved her and hated her at the same time. She tortured me and gave me painful exercises to do (which I did faithfully). I would not be walking today or using my arm without a trace of injury if it were not for Mary Ellen Diffily. One day she would be Joe's therapist, too, when he would become a hospice patient.

My friends did not desert me. They cooked wonderful meals that Joe could pop in the oven. They made sure we had a delicious dinner every night. They washed and pressed shirts for Joe and for my father and helped to care for my mother. There is no way that I could ever thank them for the love and care they gave to us. Friends like that are irreplaceable.

With my elderly mother in a wheelchair, and now me in a wheelchair, it was a bit crowded and comical at times in the Quinlan home. My cast-covered leg stuck straight out and was prone to bumping into things like furniture and my mother's wheelchair. Mama had a good sense of humor and we shared many laughs over it.

Meanwhile, Mary Ellen was doing her internship in Pennsylvania. She traveled over the mountain every weekend to help her dad. She traveled through many snowstorms, heavy rains and thick fogs, but she never missed a weekend. John had his own business and was living in Elizabeth, New Jersey at the time. He came every morning to help care for his grandparents and his mom. It was hardest on Joe. He continued to visit Karen twice a day, then came home and played nurse to me.

What I missed most during my rehabilitation was not seeing Karen every day. When Joe came home, he would share his visit with me, telling me if she was restless, peaceful or congested. But it was not the same as being there. After several months when I was feeling better, Joe would bring me to the nursing home on the weekends. It would be five more months before I could drive myself.

Saying Good-Bye to Mama and Papa

Long before my accident Joe and I had planned to vacation in San Francisco in August. My leg was still in a cast, my arm in a sling. I was still in a wheelchair but managing to cook. I knew Joe could use a vacation, but I didn't want to leave my mother and father alone, who needed full-time care and even the assistance of a home health aide. John and Mary Ellen encouraged us to go. John offered to come every morning before the health aide left. Mary Ellen would be there on the weekend. My mother was the one that insisted we go. Mama said, "Julia, you and Joe need to get away. Please go." Reluctantly, I agreed.

The night before we were to leave, my mother and I talked about the trip. She was so happy that we decided to go. "Mama," I said, "if you are sleeping in the morning, I will not wake you. You need your rest, so we'll say our good-bye now." She replied, "Have a wonderful trip." Joe and I helped her get ready for bed and said goodnight.

My mother was awake when the aide arrived in the morning. When we were ready to leave, the aide was bathing my mother. I didn't want to disturb her or invade her privacy, so I just called in, "Mama, we are leaving, see you when we get back. Take care. John will be here before the aide leaves." Mama called back, "Have a good time, don't worry about me." For some reason that I cannot explain, I stopped at the front door, turned to Joe, and said, "Honey, wait one minute, I'm going to say good-bye to my mother." I went into her bedroom and sat and talked to her for a minute or two, then kissed her. Once again, she said, "Don't worry about me. You and Joe have a good time. I'll see you in a week." Then we left for the airport.

We were unable to get a direct flight to San Francisco; we had a stopover at O'Hare in Chicago. While we were waiting to board the connecting flight, I heard my name announced over the loudspeaker: "Julia Quinlan, please come to the desk, you have a phone call." I know my heart stopped, as I stood frozen. My first thought, of course, was that Karen was dying or had died, without Joe and me at her side. I don't know how I made it to the phone.

"Hello, this is Julia Quinlan."

A doctor on the other end said, "I'm sorry to tell you that your mother had a massive stroke this morning. She is in the hospital. Your father and son, John, are with her. I understand that you are the person designated to make decisions for her. As I mentioned, it was a massive stroke, and I doubt she will survive. If it should be necessary, do you want me to resuscitate her? ...Julia, are you there? Do you want me to resuscitate?"

I stood there, numb. For the second time in my life I was asked to make a life-or-death decision for someone I dearly loved. I knew my mother's wishes. She and my father had both expressed them many times after visiting Karen. They would never want to be left in that condition, and they would never want to put me through the agony of watching either of them suffer a long and painful death. "No, doctor, do not resuscitate—that would be my mother's wish."

"Thank you, Julia. John has called your daughter. He has been with his grandfather all day. Good-bye."

There was only one seat available on the next flight to the airport in Newark. A flight attendant overheard my conversation with Joe and offered me her seat. She said, "I can take another flight home." How could I ever thank this stranger?

On the long journey home my thoughts turned to that morning. How could this happen? Mama was fine when I left and seemed genuinely happy that I was making the trip. How I wished I had been there. I knew though, that there would have been nothing I could have done for her. It was a massive stroke. Thankfully, John was with her.

It was late in the evening when Joe and I arrived at the hospital. John said, "Grandpa sat at her bedside all day, talking to her and crying. He would not leave her side." Mary Ellen called me aside and said, "Grandma is in a coma. There is no hope of recovery." I looked at my mother, and she was at peace. I was grateful she was not in pain. I knew that I had made the right decision. This is how she would have wanted it.

As I leaned over to kiss my mother, my thoughts returned to the morning when I had said good-bye to her. I was thankful that I listened to my intuition. John said she had the stroke shortly after we left the house. I looked at my mother again. She was ninety years old and now she was gone. Then I turned and looked at my father: his partner of over sixty years was gone. More than ever I wanted to make his life as happy as possible. But that was not to be.

Back home, my father was bewildered and lost without Grandma (as he called her). His children, grandchildren,

Joe nor I could make him truly happy. I took him shopping, took him to visit Karen, cooked his favorite dishes, but I could not fill his emptiness.

Every afternoon my father would go to his bedroom and nap. Before lying down, he would kneel at the side of the bed to pray, as he and Grandma always did. Every day he would say the same prayer: "Lord, take me home, so I can be with Grandma again." Then he would add, "And you can marry us again, and we'll be together forever." It was a low time in my life. I didn't know how to reach him.

Papa continued his daily walks. One afternoon in February 1984 he fell while walking in front of the house. He broke his arm, but was not seriously hurt. While he was in the hospital a series of tests were done. They found some minor problems that could worsen without treatment. They also thought Papa would benefit from further testing. We talked it over and together asked the doctor many questions. Papa was very alert and capable of making his own decisions. But I could tell he had lost his desire to live. He refused further testing and from that moment on he didn't help with his recovery. After about a week Papa's prayers were answered. He lived only six months after my mother died. He was ninety-three. He was now home where he longed to be, with Grandma. They should have put "died from a broken heart" on his death certificate.

PART TEN : SAYING GOOD-BYE TO KAREN

After my father died, I spent more time at the nursing home. Often I would meet Joe there, and we would spend time together with our daughter. Karen was growing weaker every day. Her body was skeletal. Out visits became more and more difficult. I watched Karen's slow deterioration. She looked tired, and her skin was drawn taut. She would have been unrecognizable to a stranger. We both wondered how long she could go on like this.

Joe and I started to prepare ourselves for the inevitable. We had purchased a family plot in Gate of Heaven Cemetery in Hanover, New Jersey, several years prior, and we had already made funeral arrangements and covered all the necessary details that needed to be attended to at a time when our thoughts would be elsewhere. We hoped to keep the arrangements as secret as possible. The management at the cemetery was most cooperative. They had no desire to be inundated with photographers and reporters.

But our little fighter lingered on. On March 29, 1984,

we celebrated her thirtieth birthday with a Mass in her room. We continued our daily visits and celebrated another Christmas at her bedside. It seemed incredible that April 15, 1985, would be the tenth anniversary of her accident and the fifth anniversary of the hospice founded in her name. I had no way of knowing that 1985 would be the year of her death.

On the morning of June 7, 1985, I received a phone call from the nursing home that Karen had developed pneumonia. Joe immediately called Mary Ellen and John. By the tone of his voice, they knew it was serious. We had all noticed a rapid deterioration over the prior weeks.

While Joe drove, my mind was racing. I wanted to shout, "Go faster! Go faster!" But I couldn't. Instead, I prayed, "Dear God, please don't let it happen now, let her hold on a little longer. I want to be with her."

When we reached the nursing home, we rushed upstairs to her room, not knowing what condition we would find Karen in. Her breathing was labored and she was sweating from her high fever. Her vital signs were failing.

We called our friend, Father Tom. When he arrived, we prayed at her bedside. Praying for my child to die was something I never thought I could do. But, for some reason, this time I knew it was time to let go. I knew death would be a blessing for her. Once again, she would be free.

Later in the day, Father Quinlan and Paul and Maria Armstrong joined us in our vigil. No antibiotics were administered, although a non-prescription drug was given to reduce the fever. It seemed she was in more distress now than at any other time in the last ten years. We took turns sitting with Karen, so she would not be alone day or night. She still was not ready to give up. For five days and four nights, we maintained our vigil. Food was delivered to us. The staff made us as comfortable as possible. Doctor Wolf and the nurses were supportive to the very end.

The sheriff's office was notified. A guard was placed at her door and additional guards were added later. The press held a vigil of their own, waiting for Karen to die. I felt their presence and sensed their anxiety. It gave me an awful feeling, yet I knew they had a job to do. In some ways, Karen belonged to the world. It was important for them to report how and when she died. I was aware people all over the world were praying for Karen and us, and I welcomed their prayers.

Around 5:30 P.M., June 11, Joe, Father Tom and I were standing around her bed, waiting for dinner to arrive when someone called, "The pizza is here." As they started to leave I said, "I'm staying."

"You'll just be outside the door," Father Tom said.

"No," I replied. "I'm not leaving."

Something told me to stay. When I was alone with my daughter, I held her twisted hands in mine and prayed the Memorare.

Remember, O most Gracious Virgin Mary,
that never was it known that anyone who fled
to your protection, implored your help,
or sought your intercession was left unaided.
Inspired by this confidence, I fly to you,
O Virgin of Virgins, my mother.
To you I come; before you I stand,
sinful and sorrowful.

O Mother of the Word Incarnate,
despise not my petitions
but in your mercy, hear and answer me. Amen.

I knew death was imminent. After several minutes I called the guard, "Tell them to come immediately." As we stood around her bed I continued to hold her hands, while Joe wiped her forehead. Suddenly, she was gone.

Karen's long struggle finally ended.

Father Tom, said it best, "The moment of her death was one of great reverence and a sense of loss. No matter how much we anticipated it, the moment of truth was a new moment."

For ten years I prayed that I'd be with my daughter when her life ended. God, in his goodness, answered my prayers. Her struggle was over, but her memory would live on. Her short life served a meaningful purpose.

We each said our good-byes separately. When I kissed my daughter for the last time, I thanked God for blessing me with this beautiful child and for the twenty-one happy years we shared, as well as the ten painful ones.

At six o'clock that evening Doctor Wolf arrived at the nursing home. Doctor Goode, the state's medical examiner, was already in her room. Around 7:30 P.M., Doctor Wolf pronounced her dead.

Paul, Father Tom and Doctor Wolf met with the press. This was their statement:

"Miss Quinlan developed pneumonia five days ago. She died of respiratory failure following acute pneumonia. We ask the press to respect the family's wishes, which is to be left alone to mourn the loss of their daughter in private."

Joe and I drove home in silence. What do you say to one another when you just watched your child die? It left a terrible void in my heart. There was no way to fill that void. And I really did not want to.

The Final Farewell

Karen's funeral Mass was held in Our Lady of the Lake Church in Mount Arlington, New Jersey, where so many important events of her life took place: baptism, Communion, confirmation and the final farewell.

It was a beautiful Mass of Resurrection. Father Tom (now Monsignor Trapasso) was the main celebrant. Father Quinlan, Monsignor Lasch and Father Catoir concelebrated. In his homily, Father Tom said,

> How incredible it is that the whole world should have been at the bedside of an ordinary woman. When popes and kings die, the world somehow becomes reverently silent. Karen Ann had drawn the same attention and assured us that she had fulfilled her mission. She is at peace. I'm certain that millions of people shed tears for the girl they had come to know and love simply as Karen. To most, Karen became the one human being whose human life was not only in the hands of God, but also in human hands and their technology.

"She was a very vibrant and energetic person," said Karen's best friend, Ginny, fighting back tears. "The loyalty and strength she demonstrated to her friends came from having such a loving family."

A procession of seventy cars or more, escorted by the sheriff's men, drove to Gate of Heaven Cemetery. We requested that photographers and camera crews not be allowed near the tent, where the casket was placed on a green dais. The last moments were to be private time shared only by family and close friends.

After the funeral, at the end of the day, Mary Ellen and John drove past the house they grew up in. It held many memories and stories that they shared with their sister. It was their farewell to their sister.

They return to the old neighborhood on occasion. It was the only home we shared as a complete family.

The following day I went alone to the grave to say my final farewell. In the silence surrounding me, I spoke to my daughter,

> Karen, it is difficult for me today to accept that I will never hold you in my arms again. Death is final. But you know, Karen, I can still hear your beautiful voice singing solo at Midnight Mass. It filled the church as you sang "Away in a Manger." Karen, remember at Mom and Dad's twenty-fifth anniversary celebration when you delighted the guests as you sang "Bridge Over Troubled Water"? Whenever I hear that song, I hear your voice. Remember that time when you hurt your ankle on the ski slope and you didn't want me to know? Or the first time you were away from home was when you were a counselor at St. Regis Summer Camp? I still have a letter that one of your friends sent me when you were sick. He also sent a picture of the two of you together. Remember how you loved that green VW Bug you bought? You loved to scoot around town in it. I remember all the trips we took as a family, the days on the beach watching you serve as a lifeguard. We shared so many special times together as a family. Remember the camping trips and the summer vacations? We traveled all

over the country. They were happy times. But my great-est joy, Karen, was to watch you grow and become a beautiful caring and loving young woman. These are only a few of the memories I wanted to share with you today. You will never, never leave my heart. I think the engraving on your tombstone says it all. You are "A Precious Gift From God."

For ten years my life stood still. During those years I watched my daughter die so very slowly. She could not see me, she could not hear me, she could not speak to me. Yet my love for her grew deeper with each passing day. She was there—and then she was not.

There were days when I had no desire to continue, when I did not feel like forcing a smile or acting like noth-ing had changed.

I grieved for ten years while Karen's life hung in limbo. Now, I had to grieve all over again, for death is truly final. There would be no more visits, no more brushing her hair or pressing her nightgowns and, sadly, no more goodnight kisses. As a family, we now had to pick up the pieces and start a new life—minus one.

Yet I was one of the lucky ones. I still had my loving husband and two loving children. I decided to count my blessings, rather than feel sorry for myself. My family needed me, and I needed them, perhaps more than ever.

I responded to Karen's death differently than Joe. For him the emptiness was hardest to bear. He had visited his daughter faithfully every morning and every evening. It was difficult for him to share his feelings. Often I won-dered how many times he dried his tears before entering the house.

At times I found it difficult to remember what life was like prior to 1975, when we were a complete family. I found myself gauging time and events as before or after 1975. I literally had no conscious knowledge of what happened in our country during those years. My attention was fixated on my daughter.

Once again, my life had changed. There were many things that I needed to sort out in my own mind. My top priority was to reach out to Joe and our two children. They were also grieving. It would take time, but I knew we would be there for one another.

Remembering Karen

Shortly after Karen's passing, Joe returned to work, and Mary Ellen and John went on with their lives. The house was still. Though I had only just buried my oldest child, I finally felt a certain calm. I felt at peace, because I knew Karen was now at peace. Her struggle was over.

As I sat alone in the house reflecting on Karen's final moments and the week following, I realized I was totally drained of energy. The past ten years had taken their toll. I started to look through old photo albums, cards and newspaper articles written about her. I read through some of the thousands of letters we received from people across America and Europe. I wondered how many prayers were offered for this young woman whom these people never knew but still cared for. I was alone, but I did not feel alone. I was surrounded by memories.

I came across one letter in particular that touched me profoundly. It came from a young man who had known Karen when she was a teenager. He had met Karen at Christ House, a place where young people could share and learn more about their faith. The group met on Friday evenings, and she and a few friends sang and played music together. Karen and the young man became fast friends, but went their separate ways. But later they met again in the summer of 1972, when they both got jobs as counselors at St. Regis Camp on Long Island. Shortly after he heard of Karen's accident, he wrote me the following letter:

> I met Karen at the Christ House. I was quite shy then, yet Karen reached out to me. I had no idea the beautiful person who touched my life then would touch millions of lives in days to come.
>
> We were to meet again in the summer of 1972 at Camp St. Regis. Karen shared my surprise at our meeting again, so unexpectedly and out of the blue. That summer we dated awhile and became close friends and shared memories. It was a time I remember well, and that had a great impact on my life and Karen was a large part of it. She had a certain something or quality that is difficult to put in words, yet somehow I sensed it when I first met her. She was special.

As I read through more letters like these and turned the pages of more photo albums, I found peace and comfort. Especially when I came across the baby pictures. First of Karen with her round face and dimpled chin. Then came Mary Ellen also with a round face and a big clump of black hair on her head. Then came John—he was so large at birth. Then there was a picture of Karen holding her baby brother (he didn't look like he was enjoying it), and Mary Ellen sitting on the sofa. There were pictures of them at Christmas, amazed at the glitter of lights and the toys.

There were so many pictures of the trips we took every summer. Joe and I would get up about two in the morning, pack the station wagon and then wake the children. Before dawn we would be off to Vermont, New Hampshire or Maine. Or we would head in the opposite direction and visit the Carolinas or Williamsburg. Sometimes we went camping. I even learned to sleep in the tent with the family and not in the back of the station wagon! That was quite and accomplishment for good ol' mom. There were countless pictures of Karen—playing racquetball, trying out for cheerleading or getting ready to go skiing. She loved both winter and summer sports. She was my active child. She also loved to sing, play the piano or just curl up and read. The three children always seemed to have a book in their hands.

Karen was the apple of her grandparents' eyes. She enjoyed being with them and telling them stories about school or her latest boyfriend. Often she took them for a ride in her little green Bug and out for ice cream.

There was still another facet of Karen: independent and opinionated. They are both good qualities to have. How fortunate it was for us that she shared many of her opinions with us! Karen, Mary Ellen and I had long discussions on all sorts of topics—and yes, some even on life and death. I was fortunate for those long talks and for Karen's outspoken ways. It helped us to make that fateful decision in 1976. *We knew what our daughter would have wanted.*

PART ELEVEN : LIFE AFTER HER DEATH

A Prayer for Karen's Birth Mother

THE FIRST ANNIVERSARY OF KAREN'S DEATH was celebrated at a private Mass with Father Tom, Father Quinlan, family and friends. At this Mass Father Tom shared with us that Karen died on the anniversary of his ordination to the priesthood. He said, "I've always felt that the case was a significant part of my priesthood and to have Karen die on my anniversary made it more significant." Since that first Mass we have continued to celebrate Karen and Father Tom's anniversary at a private Mass for family and friends. It is a wonderful way to thank God for her life and all that her short life accomplished.

At this particular Mass I have always said a silent prayer of thanksgiving for Karen's birth mother. I pray that somehow in her heart she knew or knows that I would be forever grateful for the courage and selflessness she demonstrated when she gave her daughter up for adoption. I cannot imagine the pain she must have felt in her heart, when she handed over her newborn child. I can only hope time has assuaged her pain, and that perhaps, if she did know (or does know) that Karen was her daughter the knowledge of Karen's life, death and effect on the world, brings her some comfort.

When Karen was dying, I thought, "How wonderful it would have been for her birth mother to hold her daughter once again."

During our ordeal, because of all the publicity surrounding the case, I received many letters from women who were certain that Karen was their daughter. But the facts did not add up. For whatever reason her birth mother never did come forward. I know that someday she, Karen and I will be together and then she will understand the words on Karen's tombstone—the first words I ever heard while holding her.

Joe and I Begin to Celebrate Life
Shortly after Karen's one-year anniversary in heaven, Joe decided to take an early retirement. Our ten-year struggle had been physically and emotionally exhausting. We needed time together. We also needed time to spend with Mary Ellen and John. For ten years their lives stopped too, and they deserved some joy, happiness and attention from their parents.

On September 22, 1986, Joe and I celebrated our fortieth wedding anniversary. Joe and I strongly felt the need to celebrate a happy occasion with family and friends. We were married at a very young age, but we took our marriage vows seriously. Now we had the opportunity to renew our vows and profess our love and commitment to one another in the presence of God, family and friends. It was particularly meaningful to have Mary Ellen and John at our side to share this special day.

Our celebration started with a Mass at our parish church, St. Jude the Apostle, in Hamburg, New Jersey. Our dear and devoted friend Father Tom was the main celebrant with Father John Quinlan and our pastor Father O'Rourke concelebrating. Monsignor gave the homily. He spoke about our commitment to one another and to our daughter Karen. "That faithfulness is not only between husband and wife, but also family," he said.

I made an album of our life together for the occasion. The album started off with the announcement of our engagement and our wedding pictures. I also included pictures of the three children as babies, then as older children on family outings and vacations and then as they grew to be young adults.

It was a wonderful night for sharing memories. Joe and I danced into the wee hours of the morning.

The best part of the evening came when John and Mary Ellen surprised us with a second honeymoon trip to Hawaii. We spent three beautiful weeks there the following February. What a fabulously romantic place to renew our love and friendship! There were days when we did not want our dream vacation to end.

Joe's retirement was just what we needed at this time in our lives.

Seeing the World
We have always loved to travel; now we could to do so without the fear of leaving behind our loved ones. When we were planning a trip to Belgium, Joe expressed a desire to search out the Lenelle family, who he met during the

war. They befriended Joe and other servicemen during their tour in Belgium. Joe often spoke of them. He was grateful for all they did to help make their lives more endurable. It was a cold December in 1944, and the Lenelle family cooked meals, baked bread and allowed the men to relax and enjoy themselves. Joe had never forgotten their kindness. I looked forward to meeting them.

However, after we were settled in our hotel room, Joe had a change of heart. He decided not to proceed with the search. He did not give me a reason. Instead, he became silent. Whatever those memories were that haunted him, they remained with him. I could only assume he had no desire to relive that painful time in his life. I know that he relived those many memories many times in his sleep. After that the Lenelle family was never mentioned again.

We continued our journey to Liege, a beautiful, small city with cobblestone streets, quaint little stores and, of course, delectable chocolates. We celebrated my birthday with dinner in a lovely old restaurant. Joe seemed relaxed, and I hoped the excitement of Leige helped to erase the bitter moments he experienced in Belgium.

Then we traveled to Paris, one of the most beautiful cities with its romantic boulevards and outdoor cafes. We then traveled on to England, Portugal, Austria and Germany. Each place had its own unique beauty. I loved the mountains in Austria as much as all the historic sights of London. I enjoyed our relaxing days and nights on the Costa del Sol in Portugal, just as I enjoyed the sights and sounds of bustling Munich.

After Joe and I had done a considerable amount of traveling on our own, we invited our children to join us on a trip to Ireland. For three weeks we rented a house over-looking the Irish Sea. Mary Ellen and John each brought a friend. The old house had a large fireplace in the oversized kitchen. There was a formal dining room, living room, three bedrooms plus a master suite with a balcony. The weather was uncharacteristically dry and sunny. In fact, we had daylight until about nine in the evening. We drove from the East Coast to the West Coast and stayed in a bed and breakfast. The people were friendly, the pubs were lively and the cooking was superb. We all had a wonderful time sightseeing, walking the beach and just relaxing. We even discovered where both sets of our ancestors, the Duanes and Quinlans, called home.

Joe Goes Back to Work

After a few months of retirement, Joe found he had too much time on his hands. He had always been a very active man. He loved to remodel and to build. So he and John formed a construction company and began to build homes in our area. To this day John talks about how much he learned about the building industry from his father. Having one hand was never an impediment for Joe. He used the hook or his prosthetic hand to hammer, to put up sheetrock or to drill. There was not a building task that he was not able to do. If the job seemed impossible, Joe would study it and improvise. He had developed extraordinary strength in his right hand. The progress in prosthetics was remarkable. Joe could even hold a cigarette or pick up a nail with his prosthetic hand, which was made to look as natural as possible by matching Joe's skin tone. Often people did not realize, at first, that he had an artificial hand—

it was that natural-looking. It was a blessing for Joe. He was able to do all the things he had always wanted to do.

Mary Ellen's Wedding

My life was to change again, only this time it was with joy and happiness. In November of 1992 Mary Ellen and her fiancé, Richard Forzano, were married. She was a beautiful bride, and her father was very proud to walk down the aisle with her. Her best friend was her maid of honor, and John was an usher.

Monsignor Trapasso performed the ceremony with Father Lou (a friend of Richard's). It was wonderful to see Mary Ellen smiling and happy. When she danced with her father, it brought tears of joy to my eyes. I had promised myself that I would not get too emotional and spoil my daughter's special day, and I didn't. But I made up for it when I got home.

The following day Mary Ellen placed her bridal bouquet on Karen's grave. Her sister was part of her wedding after all.

PART TWELVE : MORE WORK TO DO

Building Up the Hospice

WITH JOE WORKING AND WITH John and Mary Ellen married, I, too, needed to fill my days.

More than ever before, I threw myself into work at the hospice. Before I knew it, the program had grown remarkably. Soon we were serving three counties: Sussex and Warren in New Jersey and Pike County, Pennsylvania.

On April 15, 1995, we celebrated fifteen years of bringing care and comfort to those in the last stages of life. The community we served honored us that evening for our contribution to society in establishing the Karen Ann Quinlan Hospice and for our commitment to patients, families and the community. In honoring Joe and me, they honored Karen.

Death and Dying Conferences
While Karen was in a coma, and then after her death, Joe and I were often asked to speak at conferences relating to

the topics of "the right to die," "death with dignity," "the study of bioethics" and "euthanasia." Because of our unique and very public case, we were asked to share our story with other families that had experienced a similar situation. Doctors, nurses, ethicists and caregivers usually attended the conferences. Our basic message was that we wanted to give a "family perspective" to the health care community.

Joe and I had always enjoyed a close relationship. But by participating in these conferences, we were afforded another opportunity to share our story and memories together and learn about each other in new and different ways. We found that we worked quite well together, complemented each other and enjoyed each other's insights. Although it was difficult at times to relive the hurt, it was overall a rewarding and enlightening experience.

What was even more rewarding was that by participating in these conferences, Joe and I were also able to listen to others who were hurting deeply. We realized we were not alone—and neither were the people we were reaching out to. Over the years Joe and I heard of hundreds of similar cases that did not reach the newspapers. All of the people we met and spoke to were ordinary—they were just like us. They were just ordinary families in extraordinary situations, hoping to make the right decisions for their loved ones.

Television and Speaking Engagements
During the height of Karen's case and popularity, and even after her death, Joe and I were invited to appear on television in France, Belgium and England. I was surprised to find out how familiar the people of those countries were

with the case. But it didn't take long for me to see that Karen's picture was on the front page of their newspapers and magazines. Joe and I were recognized and approached in restaurants and on the street. Honestly, we couldn't get over it.

We appeared on television with doctors who talked openly about euthanasia and physician-assisted suicide. When we spoke in Europe, we observed that attitudes about death were different in many ways. Most Europeans did not seem to have the same fear of death as Americans appeared to. Then again, Europe in the 1970s and 1980s was still stinging from World War II and the Cold War. The memories of those conflicts were still fresh, especially for the elder populations. Death had been an ever-present fact for many of them, and therefore less taboo than it was for the relatively protected and shielded American psyche.

Working with Other Families Like Ours *

When we returned home from Europe, we continued our participation in the numerous conferences that were held on these important issues. We shared the podium with Bob and Ellie Laird, Pete Buralacchi, the father of Christine Buralacchi; Patricia Brophy and many others. We were not professional speakers. We spoke from the heart. We all shared one thing in common: We had to fight for the right of our loved one to die in peace and with dignity.

Some still felt anger. The anger was not directed at an individual doctor but at the institutions that blocked their requests to stop life-sustaining treatment. In our case St. Clare's Hospital fought us every inch of the way. Ironically,

---

All quotations in this section are from Managing Mortality Conference Notes, *University of Minnesota, July 1993.*

the legal system helped my family and other families at no cost. Our case was the nation's first public recognition that a dying patient, competent or incompetent, has the right to refuse treatment. It decided who had the right to make decisions for an incompetent loved one.

At one conference I listened to Pete Buralacchi, whose daughter Christine was involved in a serious car accident and whose prognosis was that she would forever be in a persistent vegetative state. At the time Pete was embroiled in a battle in Missouri courts over the right to end life support for his daughter. Pete wondered how anyone who had not taken his daughter to soccer games, been at her birthday parties or taught her to drive in an empty parking lot could ever presume to have more legitimate authority about the course of her medical care than he did.

Pat Brophy said she had known her husband since childhood. She knew his wishes. His brothers, sisters and aged mother agreed. Yet he spent three years in a persistent vegetative state before the Massachusetts Supreme Court granted her request to release her husband from extraordinary means.

Bob and Ellie Laird's daughter was four and a half months pregnant, when she was involved in an automobile accident. She was taken to the hospital and operated on immediately for several injuries. During the operation the baby did not survive. Additionally, Nancy lost the oxygen supply to her brain, resulting in irreversible brain damage.

At the conference Ellie said, "It took four years before we were able to discuss the futility of prolonging her life. As a family we watched as our loving, bright daughter was reduced to a mindless shell."

The stories were emotional. Our hope was that the stories would help doctors, nurses and others to grapple with the ethical and moral considerations that modern-day technology generated in trying to sustain life indefinitely.

Joe and I stressed that families must have primary decision-making authority when a loved one is not capable of making decisions. Someone at the conference made the statement, "Surely one test for who ought to have the authority to make decisions for their loved one is whether or not they will ever visit the grave or shed a tear once the lawyers and the cameras go away."

A doctor who spoke at another conference stated, "We can't graduate from medical school without knowing how to resuscitate, but we can without knowing how to help a person to die," he said. "Teach us to be good doctors. Teach us how to be as good at helping patients and their families as we are at our own specialties."

Also at these conferences, there were discussions and panels on physician-assisted suicide. Joe and I strongly disagreed with physician-assisted suicide, and did not feel that our wish for Karen to die peacefully without the use of machines was equivalent to physician-assisted suicide. Nevertheless, we listened to all the stories, and in response we felt we had an opportunity to speak further about hospice and how we care for someone who is dying. It is a different way of caring. It is done with love, compassion and support from a team of professionals—all with a strong belief in *life*. We have found that often patients do not fear death, only suffering while they live. Hospice is there to help those who are dying while they are living. Hospice workers' main objective is to control pain and suffering, not control death. Patients should die peacefully and naturally as possible, and above all, with dignity. With the support of our doctors, nurses, chaplain and volunteers, the patient and family can develop a sense of calm and peace about this natural occurrence. The support we give to families during and after their loved one's death is very important. It can be an emotional and painful experience. Unlike Doctor Kevorkian, whose goal is to assist with a person's death, a hospice is there to support the living and dying on the natural journey toward death—in God's time.

Joe and I met many wonderful people at the conferences and some strong friendships developed. But one conference will always hold a special place in my heart.

The "Twenty-Year Retrospective" Conference

On the twelfth and thirteenth of April 1996, Joe and I attended the "Twenty-Year Retrospective" Conference, which was held in Princeton, New Jersey. It was a conference to discuss and debate the impact of the New Jersey Supreme Court decision made on March 31, 1976. The conference was also set up to honor and remember the life and death of Karen.

Ethicists, doctors, lawyers and others in the health field gathered together to provide participants with an understanding of the changes in law, ethics and health decisions that resulted from this important decision.

During the conference speakers praised the decision. They discussed the legislation that was passed, the ethics committees now mandatory in hospitals and hospices and the changes in the public's outlook on death and dying.

That evening gave Joe and I an insight into the rippling effects that this historic decision had on laws and health care. When we asked to have extraordinary means removed from our daughter, we had no idea of the magnitude of that decision. Attorneys and ethicists now had a case that they could turn to. Karen became the face that the average family could relate too. Though the conference had been held twenty years later, the topics were no less relevant.

The last evening of the conference, a reception was held to honor our family. We were presented with a plaque, which read, in part:

> In tribute to their daughter and the legacy of the land-mark American case which proudly bears the name of Karen Ann Quinlan. In dedication to the Quinlan Family for the conviction, witness, courage and fidelity which affirmed the sacred role of family and caregivers in making fundamental decisions at the end of life. From a grateful national and international health care community assembled here in Princeton to honor your signal contribution this twelfth day of April, 1996.

We were humbled and honored to receive the award. We were proud to accept it on behalf of Karen. She was not aware of all the good that resulted from her accident, but nonetheless it was her life and death that spurred all the changes that we take for granted today. We were just her instruments.

I will never forget that conference. It will always have a special meaning for me. For neither Joe nor I knew that just two months later he would be diagnosed with cancer. It was to be the last conference—the last event—we would share together.

PART THIRTEEN : JOE'S FINAL DAYS

In the cold winter of 1996, Joe and I decided it was time to head for a warmer climate. We were fortunate to find an available condo in Florida. The weather was not as sunny and warm as usual, because it was an exceptionally cold winter. Nevertheless, Joe and I were just content not to be driving or walking on icy and snowy roads. Because Sussex County had so many beautiful rolling hills, we could not even walk outside without overexerting ourselves, so Joe and I walked every day on the high school track, just up the road from our home. When we were in Florida, however, we took advantage of the flat land and more temperate climate.

On our first day in Florida, we settled into the condo. Then we went for our daily walk and had an early dinner in a nice restaurant. It had been a long day. The following day we felt well rested and ready for a long, long walk. After a short distance Joe felt a little tired and wanted to rest. That was strange, but I thought maybe he was still tired from the trip. The following day we had walked only a short distance when he said his leg was bothering him. He said, "You go on, Hon. I'll wait here for you."

He tried walking the following day with no success. We decided to give it a rest for a while and relax and enjoy the pool. After a few days Joe wanted to try again. He said, "I'll walk as far as I'm able and wait there for you." I didn't want to say no, because I knew he was doing it to please me. That was the last day of our walks.

Joe was very good about taking care of his health. He had a yearly checkup; his prostate exam was normal and blood pressure was stable. He had stopped smoking twenty years prior and had always maintained his weight. In short, he was in excellent health.

After we returned from Florida Joe decided to visit a doctor at the VA Hospital in Lyons, New Jersey. On his visit he told the doctor about the walking incident and the pain in his left leg. The doctor found nothing seriously wrong and suggested physical therapy three times a week. Joe went faithfully. He was not a complainer, so it was hard for me to know when he was in pain.

By the time April and May rolled around, Joe and I were ready to head back outdoors. We worked together, planting flowers and tidying the lawn. But there were signs that something was wrong. Around the end of May or early June, Joe's back started to bother him. He made an appointment with the doctor and had some tests done, but the doctor was not able to locate the cause of his back pain. Joe went back again later that June. I drove him. The doctors ordered more tests and prescribed pain medication. We were both puzzled. Why could they not find the cause of the pain? I was not satisfied and suggested he see our family doctor.

When we arrived home from our visit to the doctor, he could scarcely make it up the stairs. After lunch he rested, which was most unusual. In the evening he watched television, but he was still in pain. His medication did absolutely nothing to ease the pain. He was tired, and around ten in the evening he decided to go to bed. When he got up from the chair, he collapsed to the floor. He was unable to pull himself up with his one hand, because his strength had left him.

Together we managed to stand him up, only to have him fall again. He literally crawled to the bedroom. Somehow I gathered the strength to get him into the bed. He took the medication and hoped he would get some sleep. When I checked on him, he seemed to be more comfortable. Around three or four in the morning, he woke with severe pain. When he tried to sit up, he fell backward. I placed pillows behind him for support. He fell forward. I managed to lie him down in the bed, and then I called my family physician who said, "Get him to the hospital immediately."

I called my son. He was at the house in a matter of minutes. John has always been smaller built in stature than his father, but he was equally as strong. He picked up his dad and carried him to his car. I followed in mine.

The Diagnosis

When we arrived at Newton Memorial Hospital, the doctor was waiting for us. He examined Joe and suspected cancer of the spine. Since Newton was not equipped to handle that condition, the doctors suggested that Joe be transferred to Morristown Memorial Hospital in Morristown. While we waited for the transfer to be arranged, John called his sister and explained what had happened. Mary Ellen was to meet us at Morristown.

In the meantime, John contacted Doctor Wolf (Karen's doctor from the Nursing Home) for the name of an excellent surgeon. He recommended Doctor Richard Hodosh. When we arrived at the hospital, Doctor Hodosh examined Joe and recommended an MRI. Our worst fear was confirmed. Joe had cancer in his spine.

Joe was awake and alert. After a frank discussion with the surgeon, Joe wanted to proceed with the recommended operation fully aware of the potential complications. He was operated on that evening. We waited through the night, praying, trying to understand what was happening. Joe was such a strong man, the picture of health. I wondered why they didn't suggest an MRI at the VA Hospital. The cancer could have been detected in its early stage. I had so many questions and so much anger. But my main concern now was for my husband. I prayed that the operation would be successful.

The hours passed slowly. Finally a nurse came over and said Joe was in the recovery room. Before visiting him, Doctor Hodosh spoke to us. He said the surgery went well, and Joe tolerated the procedure well.

We stayed with Joe until he woke. We wanted to see him open his eyes, hear him speak and tell us he was all right. When we visited him in his room, he was sitting up. He felt confident that he would win this battle. He had faced adversities in the past and was able to overcome them. I prayed that he was right. Not wanting to leave Joe alone, we took turns going home to shower. We had been at the hospital for over twenty-four hours.

About a week later Joe began chemotherapy. Meanwhile, Joe fought high temperatures with no discernable source. He continued his physical therapy at the hospital, but the aim was to transfer him to the Morristown Memorial rehab center. They would not do this until he was without a fever for one or two days. There were many days when he was too fatigued to stand up. He was unable to bear weight on his left leg, and his right leg was getting weaker, but he remained optimistic.

In September he was transferred to Kessler Rehabilitation Center in Chester. The physicians at Morristown Rehab felt Joe needed more intense therapy than they could provide. Kessler had a good reputation, and we hoped there would be some improvement. It was a pleasant environment. I was able to have dinner with him in the dining room, and on nice days I wheeled him outdoors to the garden. He continued physical therapy several times a week. The goal was to teach him to transfer himself from the bed to the wheelchair and to strengthen his legs. He gave it his all, but there was no improvement.

Celebrating Fifty Years

On September 22, 1996, we celebrated our fiftieth wedding anniversary. We asked for and received permission to take Joe to a nearby restaurant to celebrate the occasion with family and friends.

We laughed, reminisced about our wedding day and shared happy memories of our life together. Joe surprised me with a beautiful necklace he had asked a friend to purchase. But that was my Joe. Even in his illness his thoughts were of me and to make our day special.

I could see he was in pain, but the good sport that he was, he wanted the evening to last forever. When we returned to Kessler, he was exhausted. But he was thankful he had had the chance to celebrate our special day outside an institutional setting.

I wish I could have read his thoughts that evening. The children and I had been his life. How do you let go? How do you accept the inevitable?

When I kissed him goodnight, I knew it would be an anniversary that would never leave my heart. For fifty years this wonderful man gave me his uncompromising love. We shared happiness together. We shared heartaches together. Through it all we never fell out of love.

Making Another Tough Decision

After several more weeks of physical therapy, he was transferred back to Morristown Memorial. They resumed chemotherapy, but I could see he was getting weaker and weaker. He was losing weight, and there was progressive weakness of both extremities, on his left side more than his right side. Joe's temperature continued to peak, and he was tested again and again to try to find the cause. The chemo was not helping him; the therapy was not making him stronger.

There comes a time when you must face the inevitable. It does not mean that you have lost hope; your hope is channeled in a different direction. We both knew it was decision time. We talked and talked; Joe said he wanted to come home. He wanted to be with his family, his dog Muggsy and Tuffy the cat. He wanted no more treatments, just palliative care. The children and I supported his decision whole-heartedly. I immediately contacted our hospice.

The doctor did not suggest hospice, so we had to approach him. We were ready to face reality; the doctor was not. This is a problem that is not uncommon in hospice. Too often a patient is entered into the program when it is too late to take full advantage of their services. Sometimes just days, sometimes even hours before death. This is not hospice care. It is a crisis situation.

I would not allow this to happen to my husband. He wanted to come home, where I could care for him. He wanted a death free from burdensome procedures. He wanted to be free from as much pain as possible and to be included in decisions about his life and death.

Joe Comes Home to Live

The children and I rearranged the furniture so Joe's bed could be placed in front of the sliding glass door in the living room. The hospice had everything ready for his arrival. The hospital bed was delivered and all the equipment he would need was in place.

I waited anxiously for his arrival. When they brought him into the house and transferred him to the bed, I was thankful that he arrived safely. He was tired, but he had that beautiful shy smile that told me he was happy to be home. I looked at this wonderful man, and I was thankful that he would be able to enjoy the beauty of his home, the rolling hills, the vivid colors of the autumn trees.

The weather was warm, and we were able to have him join us for a barbeque on the deck. He enjoyed the sunshine and the fresh air. I wanted him to fully enjoy whatever time he had left with us.

In the days that followed my life once again changed in wonderful and new ways. I became my husband's caregiver. Tracy, the hospice nurse, taught me how to do things I never believed I was capable of. There were many times that I bathed him, changed the bedding and pulled him up in the bed to make him more comfortable. It was done with love and gratitude. I felt blessed every day that I could care for my husband. It was a gift.

Our Last Thanksgiving

With a very heavy heart I prepared the traditional festive dinner, as well as all of Joe's favorite desserts—coconut custard pie and apple pie. We were joined by Paul and Maria Armstrong. Paul and John helped Joe to the dining room table. When we were all seated, we held hands and thanked God for this very special Thanksgiving Day.

Joe was not able to sit at the table for the entire meal. Paul and John helped him back to bed. But because of the way we had set the hospital bed up, he was still able to see us and join in the conversation. We talked, laughed and shared memories of the bond that brought us together.

When they all left, I sat with Joe, and we talked until he fell asleep. I had much to be thankful for. Preparing the meal was a labor of love. To have Joe join us at the table was more than I ever dreamed could happen.

Joe was tired the following day. His temperature was slightly elevated. In spite of it, he had his usual smile for the nurse, the aide and the physical therapist. I can still hear his gentle voice saying thank you after every visit.

On December 4, the physical therapist, Mary Ellen Diffily, came for her usual session. As a eucharistic minister from our parish, she also brought Communion to us on her visits. This meant a lot to Joe. His faith had always been an important part of his life.

As I write this I feel like I am standing at Joe's bedside. It is that vivid in my mind. The therapist stood on the right side of the bed, and I stood on the left side. As I usually did, I rubbed his right leg and arm as we talked. He looked at me in a strange way and said, "Do that again." I rubbed his leg for the second time and he said, "I don't feel that." I rubbed it a third time; he didn't feel it. I continued to his thigh and chest. It was not until I reached the upper part of his chest that he felt my touch. Our eyes met. We did not speak. There was no need for words. We both knew it would only be a matter of days.

That afternoon when John visited his dad, they talked privately. I have no knowledge of what was said. I would not invade their privacy. Upon leaving, John told me he was going to visit a local funeral home. His father was ready to accept his death. John wanted to be sure all the arrangements were made in advance. He suggested that Mary Ellen and I join him.

Saturday was a rainy day. I asked Mary Ellen to accompany me to the funeral home. She looked puzzled, but agreed. We talked to the director and made funeral arrangements. I knew the time was near. I felt Mary Ellen did not.

When we arrived home, a few close friends were visiting Joe. I offered to put the tea kettle on while they set the table for lunch. I was standing at the entrance of the dining room talking to Mary Ellen, when I looked at her father. "Oh, my God," I said and raced to Joe's side. As I rubbed and kissed his face, he died. He died as he lived, quietly and peacefully with his family and close friends at his side. Our pastor, Father Bill Collins, came immediately to bless Joe and we joined him in prayer.

As fate would have it, the hospice nurse was on her way to visit Joe. It was a blessing. She was able to make the pronouncement and immediately arranged to have the hospital bed and oxygen removed. Then she proceeded to flush the remaining drugs down the toilet—to be certain they were accounted for. The funeral director, Paul Fergunson, was at the house in a matter of minutes after our phone call. After he took Joe, the house felt empty. I sat with my children and friends and talked about Joe's life. I never realized the full impact that he had on the lives of others. They spoke lovingly of him. They loved him deeply.

When they left, Mary Ellen and John moved the furniture back to its normal setting. However, there was nothing normal about that day. In the evening I sat alone with my thoughts. I looked around the room. Everything was in place, but all I could focus on was the hospital bed that wasn't there. Sometime that evening I fell asleep on the sofa. It was impossible for me to return to the bed that Joe and I shared all those years. I would not return to our bed for many, many months. The sofa became my refuge. Joe's presence filled the room.

As the days and months passed, I realized how fortunate I was. Joe had come home to live. We had talked. We had our meals together. We had time to say good-bye and to say "I love you" repeatedly. I had the privilege of caring for him and being at his side right to the end of his life.

The hospice experience I shared with Joe was his last gift to me. The most treasured gift. It gave us all the opportunity to give back some of the unselfish love that he showered on us. It gave our extended family and friends the chance to give back to this quiet, unassuming man the love and compassion he gave us all his life.

A Great Man Has Passed Away

Telling the world about his father was easy for my son. Doing it at his dad's funeral Mass was a struggle.

"When a great man dies, somebody ought to stand up and say something," he said of his father. "Well, a great man has passed away."

Blinking back tears, John proudly reviewed some of the defining moments of his father's life. How at nineteen Joe lost an arm during the Battle of the Bulge in World War II, earning the Purple Heart. How he built a little house on a fifty-foot lot in Lake Hopatcong that grew to accommodate his growing family. John spoke about how his father had to fight in the New Jersey Supreme Court to do what was right, and how every day for ten years he visited with Karen on his way to work and on his way home, so that she would not feel alone or abandoned. John also recalled one memory in particular: "I remember three men moving a piano, with two men on one side and Dad on the other. But more than that physical strength, he had strength of character, loyalty, compassion and common sense. He was a rock of moral certitude. We all gained by knowing Dad."

What a beautiful expression of love. The love and respect that they shared was unique.

Grieving Once Again

When Joe died, a part of me died with him. I knew I had to grieve once again. My fears, my apprehensions, were not much different from most widows. For me it was not having my soul mate to share my everyday thoughts and meals with, to sit with on the deck in the evening and just enjoy the silence of being together. It is the little things you miss most. The gentle touch, the tender caress, the smile—I can see it now. I always kidded him about his shy smile.

I knew I had to create a new existence for myself, a new place in a world that suddenly seemed uncertain. I wasn't sure I was capable of it. Nevertheless, I promised myself I would not become dependent on my children. They were grieving in their own way. They were young and I wanted them to live their own lives and enjoy them. I also knew they would always be there for me.

The following day I visited Joe and Karen's graves. I said farewell to my Buddy (as his family always referred to him), my best friend and my lover. He and his daughter were together once again.

A New Existence

In the spring of 1995 Joe and I had driven to Hilton Head, South Carolina, for a long vacation. On the drive home we spent a week in Charleston, South Carolina. It is one of my favorite cities. We took side trips to the Isle of Palms, Sullivan Island and Mount Pleasant. For me it was exciting to visit the places where my own mother spent her childhood. She had often vividly described it to me.

In the fall of 1997, nine months after Joe's death, I felt the need to revisit South Carolina. I wanted to be back where Joe and I spent our wonderful vacation. I needed the time to sort out my memories, to cry out loud, to walk the streets we walked together, to revisit the gardens and historical places. I felt the need to do this on my own, alone.

I rented a car at the airport and drove to my condo, which was located outside the city. That evening I walked to a nearby restaurant for dinner. It was the first time I had had dinner out alone since Joe's death. It was not a pleasant experience. I decided that from then on I would have lunch out and snack in my room at night. Dinners were reserved for couples.

The following day I set out on my own excursion, visiting the city and driving to the Isle of Palms. While I was there, I searched for my grandparents' home, but too much had changed. However, it was good to walk the roads (now paved) that had held happy memories for my mother.

After a few days passed, I called Joe's niece, who had recently moved to South Carolina. Penny was delighted to hear my voice. She and her husband Ted invited me to spend a few days with them. I drove down the following day with apprehension. Was I ready to talk to Joe's family? He had been their favorite uncle. As I drove, I remembered that the last time we were together was at Joe's wake.

All my fears and apprehensions vanished as soon as they opened their door. I was greeted with hugs and kisses, which were just what I needed. Much to my delight Irene, Joe's sister, his nephew Bobby and Bobby's wife Kathy, were also visiting. It was like a mini-family reunion.

Irene shared stories about her baby brother, Buddy (his family never called him Joe). She and two of his other sisters were much older, so he was like a doll to them. He was a chubby baby with a full head of blond hair. They loved to fuss over him. I felt they were glad they could share some of their memories with me. They needed that time as much as I did. It turned out to be a delightful evening of sharing.

The following day Penny took me on a tour of Savannah, Georgia. We did all the tourist things and had lunch at one of the historic restaurants. The next day I drove back to Charleston, refreshed, and continued my excursions.

Then after a relaxing evening with pleasant thoughts, I decided to visit Mount Pleasant and Sullivan Island. My mother shared many stories with me about the Sunday afternoon dinners they cooked for the men stationed there. And how they would gather around the piano and sing. It was a happy time for her. As I revisited the area where my mother spent her childhood and part of her adult life, I tried to imagine what it was like then. I knew they lived on a plantation and had a beautiful, large house. There was nothing familiar about the area. Mama would never have recognized it.

As I drove back to my condo, I knew it was time to leave. I cut my vacation short. I was anxious to come home to my loving family and Muggsy and Tuffy.

When I returned home, I visited Joe and Karen's graves the next day. Alone with my thoughts and memories, I again said farewell to my Buddy. I had promised him I would be strong and that I would make a new life for myself. I had just completed the first step in my journey.

Speaking at Conferences on My Own
About two years after Joe's death, I was invited to speak at a conference on life-and-death issues. My immediate reaction was to say no. Joe and I had worked so well together. I generally gave the talk, and he loved to participate in the

question-and-answer period. We complemented each other. I wasn't sure I could do it alone. I looked over my prior speeches, and as I read them, I realized I could give firsthand witness to making life-and-death choices.

I knew several of the other speakers, and I knew there was no need for fear. There is a certain kind of camaraderie that existed among speakers. We lent support to one another. The only fear that existed was in my mind.

Somehow I gathered enough courage to say yes. I am so glad that I did. I gave a heartfelt talk about my personal experience of Joe as a patient in our hospice. Although I had worked with hospice since day one, I never really knew how wonderful hospice was until Joe became a patient. Then I lived it every day and night for seven weeks. It was truly a blessing, not only for Joe but also for our children and me.

The first conference I spoke at was the most difficult. But it was a positive learning experience for me. To this day I continue to speak at conferences. I feel it is important to continue the dialogue on the important issues that touch the lives of all of us.

My "Buddy" is always there with me. The audience may not see or hear him, but he is there at my side to give me support when I need it.

A THIRTY-YEAR
RETROSPECTIVE (1975-2005)

I have thirty years of memories locked in my heart. They are a gift from Karen and Joe. The year 2005 will be a most memorable one. It will be the thirtieth anniversary of Karen's accident, the twenty-fifth anniversary of the Karen Ann Quinlan Hospice, twenty years since her death and the year of the publication of this book.

It is time for me to reflect on all that has happened in my life. I am now able to put things in perspective. Three decades ago I could not—the hurt was too deep.

On the early morning of April 15, 1975, I received a phone call that forever changed the path of my life. Later, as I sat at my daughter's bedside, there was no reason for me not to assume that she would wake in a day or two. She was so strong and healthy. I had read about such cases in magazines. What I did not know at the time was that she was in a deep coma and in a vegetative state. What I did not know was that our long journey had only just begun.

As I reflect on those past events, I realize there was no

way I could have stopped them from happening. It seemed that we were in the right place (or the wrong place) at the right time. Karen became the symbol of the abuse of technology in this technological age. She gave both fields, law and medicine, a case they could not avoid. She gave the public an issue that was pertinent to their lives. For the first time in history, people were made aware of the decisions that had to be made—as well as the reminder that death was imminent. Moreover, Karen's situation showed us all that what happened to her could happen to anyone at anytime.

The New Jersey Supreme Court decision on March 31, 1976, was a gift to humanity. At the time I could not fully appreciate it. For Joe and I it was a double-edged sword. We had won our case but we were going to lose our daughter. Today I concentrate on the benefits that we have all received from this landmark decision. It was there for the hundreds of cases that followed. It authenticated the rights of all to make fundamental decisions at the end of life. It reaffirmed the central role of the family in making decisions for their loved ones. As a society we place great value on the family.

The case became the central event in the national debates on death, dying and the prolongation of life that developed in the 1970s. The creation of ethics committees in hospitals, nursing homes and hospices throughout the state of New Jersey and the nation is a direct outgrowth of the landmark Quinlan decision.

Attitudes about the rights of dying patients have changed. Health professionals have also become more responsive to patients' rights. Today I believe we have a better understanding of life-and-death issues, although we have a long way to go—many families still are continuing to suffer and battle the legal system. It is still inconceivable to me that a family that is already suffering so intensely would have to go to court to fight for the rights of their loved one. Such decisions should not be made in the courts. Courts do not exist for making treatment decisions. Nevertheless, we must rely on these courts when other institutions fail us.

Because of our case, California passed the first living will legislation in 1976, known as the California Natural Death Act. Every state now recognizes a living will, a proxy or an advance directive. This document allows a patient to express their wishes about their plan of care—before a crisis situation.

In July 1991 Governor Jim Florio signed into law the New Jersey advance directives or living will. Relatives, friends or doctors should honor patients' wishes at a time when they are no longer able to speak for themselves. Joe and I were present at the signing. With the passage of legislation, conferences and public education, people became aware that life couldn't be extended beyond its term except through artificial means.

On the personal level there was the establishment of the Karen Ann Quinlan Hospice. It was a dream that became a reality. It was a dream that started when Karen was in intensive care. I felt there must be a more humane way to care for the dying. Since the founding of the hospice, I have had the privilege of watching it grow remarkably. We have extended our services to all of northwest New Jersey and Pike County, Pennsylvania. But our mission remains the same. We are there for patient and family, before, during and after death.

Care at the end of life is a personal and emotional experience. It affects all—the dying and their loved ones. Hospice assures that patients and their families receive the care they need to optimize the quality of their lives.

Last, I must reflect on my family. I must never forget that Mary Ellen and John were in their late teens when their lives changed. Throughout those ten years Joe and I made every effort to protect their privacy. However, we could not protect them from the private pain of watching their sister die a slow death. During those years they lived in their sister's shadow. My every thought and prayer was for Karen and I'm sure theirs were, too. But, they never doubted their parents' love; the bond was too strong.

Mary Ellen and John had to make decisions and face a situation in their teens that no parent would want for their children. They experienced a deep hurt, but they also learned many positive lessons. Because of this tragedy they have grown to be two loving and compassionate adults, reaching out to the terminally ill through hospice. They are almost as involved in the program as I am. The closeness we share as a family is still present. Their sensitivity and knowledge of death and its moral issues have reached a different level. It is a wonderful experience for me to be able to share my dreams and future for our hospice with them.

My life continues to revolve around family, friends and hospice. During my lifetime I have had many unexpected blessings. That day when Karen was placed in my arms at the altar was a turning point in my life. It was the beginning of a life that seems to have no ending. I know that I could never have found inner peace had I run away from what had to be done for Karen.

As a family we are able to look back on the decisions we made, and we are at peace. We did everything possible for Karen—medically, spiritually and legally. We would make the same decisions again.

As I reflect on the past three decades, I realize that it is not the last chapter in the life and death of Karen Ann Quinlan. Her life has served a purpose far greater than she ever expected and far greater than I could ever expect.

Joe and Karen's legacy will live on in the Karen Ann Quinlan Hospice and in the landmark Quinlan decision.

I will forever be grateful that as a family we had the strength and the courage to fight for what we believed in.

I do not know when my journey of love will end. My life has been filled with much joy and much sorrow. I am not sure you can experience true happiness if you have not experienced true sorrow. Somehow they are linked together. I have been blessed to experience both. My pain and my sorrow is now part of my happiness.

It is my precious gift from God.

APPENDIX A

THE LEGAL BATTLE: A CHRONOLOGY

April 15, 1975 – Karen Ann Quinlan is rushed to Newton Memorial Hospital, Newton, New Jersey.

April 24, 1975 – Karen is transferred to St. Clare's Hospital in Denville, New Jersey.

August 3, 1975 – Joseph and Julia Quinlan ask to have their daughter removed from all extraordinary means.

August 5, 1975 – St. Clare's Hospital refuses to honor their request.

September 12, 1975 – Attorney Paul W. Armstrong files papers in the Morristown County Courthouse, Morristown, New Jersey, asking that Joseph Quinlan be appointed guardian of his daughter, Karen Ann.

October 20, 1975 – Hearings begin in Morristown with Judge Robert Muir presiding.

November 10, 1975 – Judge Muir reaches his decision. It is not favorable to the Quinlan family.

November 17, 1975 – Appeal is filed with New Jersey Supreme Court.

March 31, 1976 – Supreme Court Chief Justice Richard J. Hughes writes a unanimous decision providing the appointment of Joseph Quinlan as his daughter's guardian.

April 8, 1976 – St. Clare's Hospital votes against an appeal.

April 26, 1976 – Joseph Quinlan signs a notarized release form, authorizing removal of the respirator and freeing doctors of liability.

May 19, 1976 – Karen Quinlan is successfully weaned from the respirator.

June 3, 1976 – Morris View Nursing Home votes unanimously to accept Karen.

June 9, 1976 – Karen is moved to Morris View Nursing Home in Morris Plains, New Jersey.

June 11, 1985 – Karen Ann Quinlan dies of acute pneumonia.

APPENDIX B

THE NEW JERSEY SUPREME COURT DECISION (EXCERPTS)

On March 31, 1976, guided by Chief Justice Richard J. Hughes, the New Jersey Supreme Court rendered a unanimous decision providing the appointment of Joseph Quinlan as his daughter's guardian. The decision stated:

> ...while Mr. Quinlan feels a natural grief, and understandably sorrows because of the tragedy which has befallen his daughter, his strength of purpose and character far outweighs these sentiments and qualifies him eminently for guardianship of the person as well as the property of his daughter. Hence we discern no valid reason to overrule the statutory intendment of preference to the next of kin....
>
> We therefore remand this record to the trial court to implement (without further testimonial hearing) the following decisions:
>
> 1. To discharge, with the thanks of the Court for his service, the present guardian of the person of Karen Quinlan, Thomas R. Curtin, Esquire, a member of the Bar and an officer of the court.
> 2. To appoint Joseph Quinlan as guardian of the person of Karen Quinlan with full power to make decisions with regard to the identity of her treating physicians.
>
> We repeat for the sake of emphasis and clarity that upon the concurrence of guardian and family for Karen, should the responsible attending physicians conclude

that there is no reasonable possibility of Karen's ever emerging from her present comatose condition to a cognitive, sapient state and that the life-support apparatus now being administered to Karen should be discontinued, they shall consult with the hospital "Ethics Committee" or like body of the institution in which Karen is then hospitalized. If that consultative body agrees that there is no reasonable possibility of Karen's ever emerging from her present comatose condition to a cognitive, sapient state, the present life-support system may be withdrawn and said action shall be without any civil or criminal liability therefore, on the part of any participant, whether guardian, physician, hospital or others. (*In the Matter of Karen Quinlan, An Alleged Incompetent*, Supreme Court of New Jersey, March 31, 1976, pp. 58–59)

APPENDIX C

THE POSITION OF THE BISHOP OF PATERSON, NEW JERSEY (EXCERPTS)

On November 1, 1975, Bishop Lawrence B. Casey of the Diocese of Paterson, New Jersey, issued a statement on the use of extraordinary means to sustain the life of Karen Ann Quinlan:

> "It is in the face of death that the riddle of human existence becomes acute." These words of the Second Vatican Council have a special meaning to the family of Karen Ann Quinlan, and indeed, to a host of people who have come to know about her tragic condition. Her parents have made a painful and difficult decision, to request the discontinuance of the means sustaining the continuation of her life; it is a decision which elicits the sympathy and concern of many people and which now demands the attention of the courts...

> I. Basic Assumptions
> 1. The Bishop of Paterson has the authority and competence to present the Church's teachings in this matter.
>
> ...It is with this authority and competence that I, as Bishop of Paterson, accept the responsibility and right to apply the teachings of the Catholic Church to the request for permission to discontinue the use of a respirator as an extraordinary means of sustaining the life of Karen Ann Quinlan, which request is made by her loving parents and our beloved brother and sister in Christ,

Joseph and Julia Quinlan, faithful members of the parish of Our Lady of the Lake Church, Mount Arlington, New Jersey, within the Diocese of Paterson.

2. Karen Ann Quinlan is alive…

3. What is being requested by Joseph and Julia Quinlan is not euthanasia…

4. The possibility of God's intervention in the recovery of health is not and cannot be precluded…

II. General Teaching of the Church on the Preservation of Life

Human life is God's great and first gift to each of us. We must love life and work to preserve it. When there is hope for returning a person from the threshold of death to a measure of recovery we should work to preserve God's gift of life…

III. Application of the Church's Teaching to the Case of Karen Ann Quinlan

Competent medical testimony has established that Karen Ann Quinlan has no reasonable hope of recovery from her comatose state by the use of any available medical procedures…. Therefore, the decision of Joseph and Julia Quinlan to request the discontinuance of this treatment is, according to the teachings of the Catholic Church, a morally correct decision.

…In all of this we pray for God's guidance of our society in its efforts to appreciate the precious gift of human life, and for His blessings upon the family of Karen Ann Quinlan and of all those in similar circumstances who must make their judgments based on mutual love. Finally, we pray for Karen herself that the

Lord, Who has brought her into the hearts and minds of more people than perhaps she ever dreamed, will bestow on her happiness which is the goal and purpose of all mankind.

—*+Lawrence B. Casey*
Bishop of Paterson
November 1, 1975
Feast of All Saints
Paterson, New Jersey

—*Frank J. Rodimer*
Chancellor

INDEX

AUTHOR BIOGRAPHY

Julia Duane Quinlan, mother of Karen Ann Quinlan, fought for the right to have her daughter removed from the respirator and die in a natural state with dignity. On March 31, 1976, the New Jersey Supreme Court handed down a landmark decision, affirming the right of us all to make fundamental decisions at the end of life.

Julia and her husband Joseph are coauthors of the book *Karen Ann,* written with Phyllis Battelle. They dedicated the funds from their book to establish the Karen Ann Quinlan Hospice in loving memory of their daughter.

Julia is a well-known and respected speaker. She has been a guest speaker at numerous conferences across the country on ethics, end-of-life care, hospice and the historic importance of the Quinlan decision. Julia has appeared on national talk shows and news broadcasts and on television in Europe and Asia.

The senate and general assembly of New Jersey have recognized Julia for her achievements in health care. She has received the New Jersey Hospice Community Leader Award and was included in *People* magazine's 1999 Special Anniversary issue under "Profiles in Courage."

Her efforts over the last two decades have been in the establishment of local community health initiatives in northwest New Jersey and Pennsylvania. She currently serves as Chairman of the Board of Governors of the Karen Ann Quinlan Hospice.

Julia resides in Wantage, Sussex County, New Jersey. Her son John, daughter Mary Ellen, and son-in-law Richard are also Sussex County residents.